Best of Disc Art 1

RotoVision

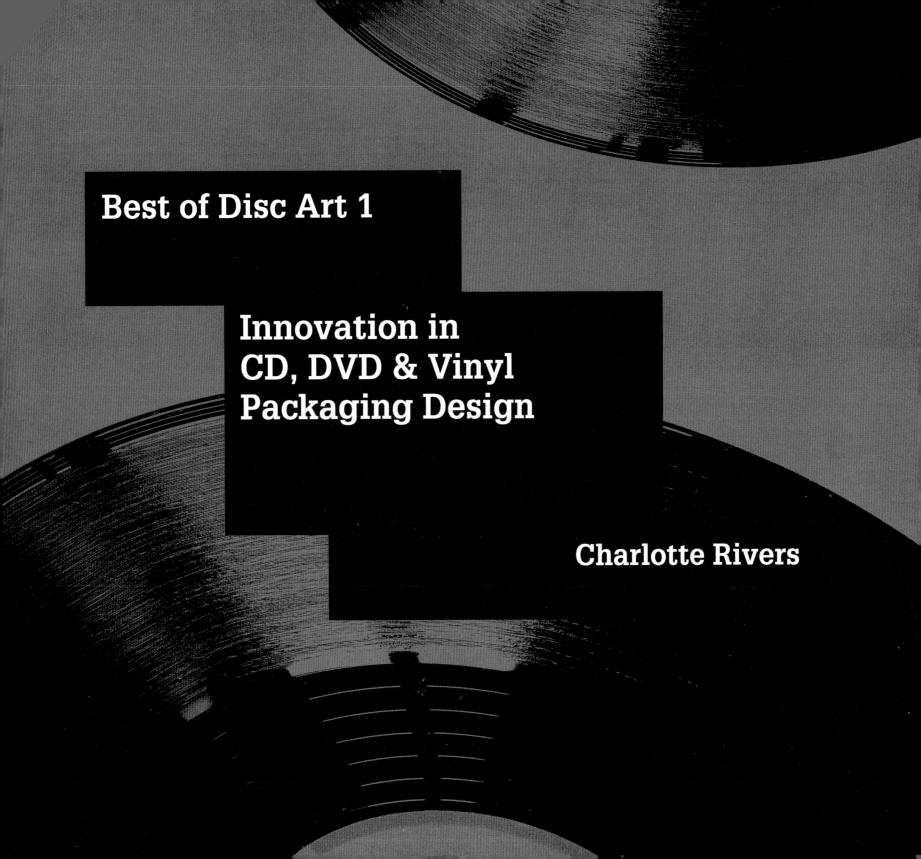

Best of Disc Art 1

Innovation in CD, DVD & Vinyl Packaging Design

Charlotte Rivers

A RotoVision Book

Published and distributed by RotoVision SA
Route Suisse 9
CH-1295 Mies
Switzerland

RotoVision SA
Sales and Editorial Office
Sheridan House, 114 Western Road
Hove BN3 1DD, UK

Tel: +44 (0)1273 72 72 68
Fax: +44 (0)1273 72 72 69
www.rotovision.com

10 9 8 7 6 5 4 3 2 1

ISBN: 978-2-940361-92-2

Art Director: Jane Waterhouse
Designer: Lisa Båtsvik-Miller

Reprographics in Singapore by ProVision Pte.
Tel: +65 6334 7720
Fax: +65 6334 7721

Printed in Singapore by Star Standard (Pte) Ltd.

Contents

CD

DVD

Vinyl

Introduction

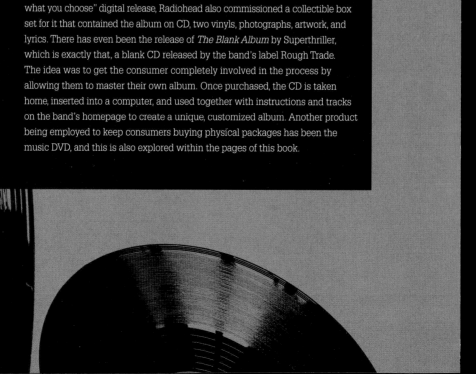

Having written *CD-Art* in 2002 and *DVD-Art* in 2005, the idea with *Best of Disc Art 1* is to combine the two to create a book that considers fresh, new examples of innovative packaging design in those areas. In addition, *Best of Disc Art 1* also looks at vinyl packaging, which, despite some doubters, is still going strong today. Together these three formats, and the packaging that is designed around them, provide us with examples of some of the most exciting graphic design being produced around the world.

In terms of the music industry, the past few years have once again seen much change. The way we choose, buy, and listen to music has shifted dramatically. Downloads are increasing, physical sales are decreasing, record stores are going bankrupt, and some artists are taking things into their own hands and selling their music to fans for as much or as little as they choose to pay. All these developments have led to much speculation about the future of the industry and how it will adapt to the different ways in which we consume music now and in the future.

That all sounds a bit gloomy, but is it? Can the traditional music store survive if it takes steps to adapt? Will vinyl, which is currently experiencing a revival, surprise us all and live on beyond the CD like it has the cassette? Or will both CD and vinyl continue to survive together? Are interactive e-books really here to replace the traditional CD booklet or are they simply giving digital music consumers the same buying experience as a physical music consumer? At the moment none of these questions can be answered because, for now, the physical and digital exist together. It is this that *Best of Disc Art 1* aims to celebrate with global examples of CD, DVD, and vinyl packaging, together with examples of how designers are taking on the "packaging" challenge of the increasingly popular digital format.

There is no escaping the facts. In the US CD sales for the first quarter of 2007 were 20 percent lower than the same period in 2006, and in the UK sales fell by 10 percent in the first half of 2007. So how can designers and the music industry address this? One thing is that designers now have to work harder to encourage people to buy physical music, or alternatively look at the opportunities that the new digital format provides them with, in terms of design. If we look at the first challenge of designing for the physical format, there are some great recent examples to cite.

Big Active has been responsible for some of the most noted, including Beck's do-it-yourself *The Information* cover involving stickers and an online gallery, and the 2007 release for Athlete, *Beyond the Neighborhood*, for which there was a limited-edition album version, which came housed in a debossed hardback cover book. The work of Non-Format for the LoAF label releases continues to be some of the best around, combining music, art, and fantastic design to produce memorable and collectible packaging. And despite *In Rainbows* being a "pay what you choose" digital release, Radiohead also commissioned a collectible box set for it that contained the album on CD, two vinyls, photographs, artwork, and lyrics. There has even been the release of *The Blank Album* by Superthriller, which is exactly that, a blank CD released by the band's label Rough Trade. The idea was to get the consumer completely involved in the process by allowing them to master their own album. Once purchased, the CD is taken home, inserted into a computer, and used together with instructions and tracks on the band's homepage to create a unique, customized album. Another product being employed to keep consumers buying physical packages has been the music DVD, and this is also explored within the pages of this book.

On the flip side, we have also seen some great examples of designers embracing the digital format and all the new, exciting design opportunities it provides. There is of course the e-book, which is becoming more and more popular. It is most commonly available to users as a bundle on iTunes, so when they purchase an entire artist album, they then get an e-book, which is downloaded together with the music to the user's iTunes library. Big Active took full advantage of the digital format with its artwork for The Enemy's *We'll Live and Die in These Towns* album. Based on railway departure boards, each time a new track is played the track details change, as a train announcement would, on the user's iPod screen. In the US the release of a series of e-books by The Gorillaz, available exclusively with iTunes, not only got them profiled on the iTunes front page and drove traffic to the band's own page within the store, but also enabled them to give the user access to something extra with their purchased music download.

The design of music and film, or moving image, packaging has traditionally provided designers with a vehicle to experiment, try out new things, and take risks. It is this freedom and opportunity that enables designers to create the work that they want to rather than having to follow a tight brief. To look at this thriving area of design, *Best of Disc Art 1* has been divided into three main areas of focus. Firstly Form, which looks at the physical side of CD, DVD, and vinyl packaging from the many and varied shapes and sizes that discs and vinyl can be packaged in, to the materials that can be used, and the different printing and finishing techniques employed by designers to add character and differentiation to a package. Then there is Content, which looks at artwork within the packaging and how designers work with artists (from up-and-coming photographers and illustrators to highly established image makers) to create stunning artwork.

This chapter also explores the art of typography within disc and vinyl packaging. The final chapter is Extending the Experience, which considers ways in which designers can extend the user's buying experience both physically and digitally. From including physical added extras, such as stickers and badges, to the aforementioned e-book made available with some download purchases.

Best of Disc Art 1 covers an extensive range of global work. Each example shows how the designer has fulfilled their CD, DVD, or vinyl packaging brief to create a memorable and marketable product that communicates, in whatever way is most appropriate, the content within. Whether designing for CD, DVD, or vinyl, all three formats provide creatives with a great design opportunity because, as with any packaging project, there is the product design (what casing to use, what materials to use), and then there is the editorial design (the cover, booklet, photographic layouts). In other words, there is the opportunity to design in 2D and 3D, with the aim of giving the user a unique and memorable experience.

Charlotte Rivers

Form

01

The following chapter explores the many ways in which the designer can differentiate a CD, DVD, or vinyl package through form. From a package's shape to its size or tactility, this is an area of the overall package design that can only be experimented with should the client and budget allow.

Thankfully many do, giving designers and manufacturers the opportunity to experiment and find alternatives to traditional disc packaging, whatever its format. The following pages show how designers are using a growing number of stocks or unusual materials within their designs, from uncoated board to clear vinyl.

There are also examples of different ways in which design solutions force the user to interact with a package in a possibly unfamiliar way, whether through the use of a bellyband or sticker to seal a package, or by housing a CD within a foldout poster package.

Finally, this chapter looks at the ever-increasing ways in which designers can customize and manipulate the materials they use, from die-cutting and foil blocking to using handheld rubber stamps.

Materials

PowWow

Sopp Collective created the packaging for
PowWow, an innovative series of 10 CD and
download releases. Each album features an
emerging band from the Australian pop scene.
"The name and design had to reflect the concept
of creating a series featuring new and exciting
artists," explains designer Katja Hartung. "We
needed some point of differentiation for each
release while creating a strong visual identity
for the project overall. In terms of production,
we also had to work around keeping the cost
low despite the small quantities for each limited
edition." Each sleeve also has a small Feral Media
stitched "label" sewn into its spine. This label
concept, previously created for all Feral Media
releases, adds a recognizable label standout
without encroaching on the artist's cover
surface. Custom premanufactured boxboard
sleeves were used to house the CDs and each
release is screen printed in one spot color,
matching the color of the CD inside.

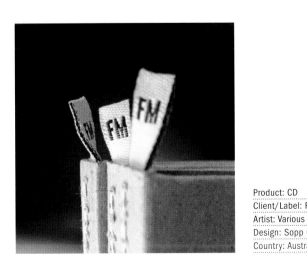

Product: CD
Client/Label: Feral Media
Artist: Various
Design: Sopp Collective
Country: Australia

Materials

Mixtape Classics

Peter and Paul designed this packaging with
a "typical music packaging brief—create
something that relates to the music, on
a shoestring budget," inspired by the title
Mixtape Classics. Recreating the look of an
audio cassette on its former rival (vinyl), meant
taking a sideways view of vinyl records and the
implications of their much-discussed demise
(much like that of the cassette). "We kept the
typography quite utilitarian, and referenced
the sticker sets that you got with each blank
cassette to create the record title," explains Paul
Reardon. The center of the records—limited
to a run of 500—were laser cut in the shape of
a tape spool, by utilizing a 7in "dink" (the bit that
fits in the middle) to create the first ever 12in—
in a medium which has enjoyed some 30-odd
years in various forms—to play like a 7in.

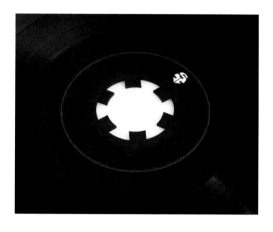

Product: Vinyl
Client/Label: SWAG
Design: Peter and Paul
Country: UK

Men-An-Tol

Luke Powell and Jethro Haynes created the all black CD packaging for this debut EP. "We all decided that the packaging should have some mystery about it," explains Powell. "We wanted people to be drawn to the object through intrigue rather than a loud graphic statement… Finally, when you take the CD out of the case you notice the whole of the inside is printed gold, giving the object an arcane feel, like you've found a lost artifact." Today Sans Extra Light typeface has been used for its quite modern feel and its several characters, like the ampersand and uppercase W, that are reminiscent of older font styles. "This inability to give the font a clear place in time was important in our choice," explains Powell. The limited run of 200 CDs was sold through various independent record stores around London. The sleeve is made from black Plike card (a rubberized plastic-like card) with the type printed in a gloss black so that it can only be seen clearly when held at an angle.

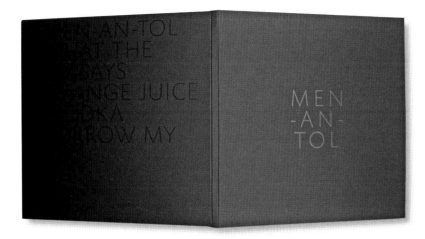

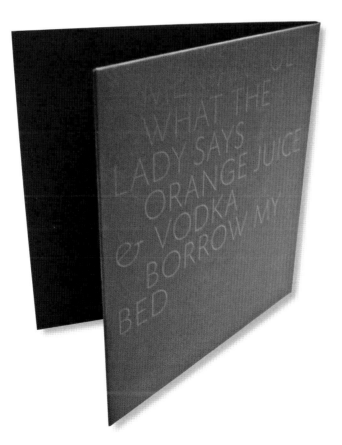

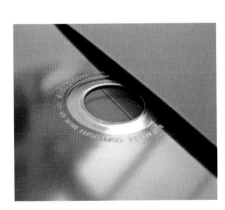

Product: CD
Client/Label: Static Caravan
Artist: Men-An-Tol
Design: Jethro Haynes with Hudson-Powell
Country: UK

Put On Your Best Dress

In this 60-minute mix of 1960s Jamaican music, the records were selected and mixed by J. Max Brill; the project was initiated by Gimme 5 to reflect Brill's love of Ska and Rocksteady. Oscar Wilson designed the package as something simple that would complement the music, but not detract from it. As all the music on the mix was recorded from original 7in vinyl singles, the CD was manufactured to resemble a 7in vinyl single, in black plastic with etched grooves. It is packaged in a die-cut white cardboard sleeve that reveals the central label (purely typographic) artwork just like a traditional 45rpm record. Wilson has used Century as the title font, with Classical Garamond for the body text (accented with italic Cataneo). "The brief was very open, but we discussed the idea of trying to create a piece of packaging that wasn't tied stylistically to any particular time period or musical genre," he explains. The CD was distributed free at a London clothes store and independent music café.

Product:	CD
Client:	Gimme 5 UK Ltd
Artist:	Various, mixed by J. Max Brill
Design:	Studio Oscar
Country:	UK

The Was

"The idea for the design of the sleeve came from corporate art," explains David Bowden. "I branded the band as I would brand a company, with logo inspiration coming from the 1940s and 1950s automotive industry. The images associated with the band were designed to be pieces of corporate art; if Make Model were a large automotive company, what would they hang on the walls of their offices and homes…? This idea runs through the whole campaign, taking the vortex motif and creating it in different ways. Here it is made of paper streamers." The logo has been set in a version of Gill Sans, with extra-wide spacing, in a bold, angular lozenge device. It was designed to sit as easily on a letterhead as it would on a record sleeve. A heavy off-white colorplan with a buckram emboss stock has been used to achieve a muted color.

Product: Vinyl
Client/Label: EMI
Artist: Make Model
Design: Zip Design
Country: UK

Materials

Malibu Stacy

pleaseletmedesign created this EP package, using a plain white digipak, and then separately producing rolls of adhesive tape that contain all the band's information, such as titles of songs, bar codes, and catalog numbers. It then applied the tape by hand to the packages. All the leftover tape was used to promote the band in the street and during its tour. Avant Garde typeface was used for its vintage style. The CD was printed in a limited run of 1,000, each of which was numbered by hand.

sh sh //01
peniche praia //02
grasshopper green //03
sex in malibu //04
morning trouble (in a coffee cup) //05

www.malibustacy.com

BC 0447

Product: CD
Client/Label: 62TV
Artist: Malibu Stacy
Design: pleaseletmedesign
Country: Belgium

Form

Butt, Sweat & Tears

"I was asked by a friend to join an experiment whereby he asked me, and 11 other people, to create a mix CD, make 12 copies, then mail a copy to each of his friends," explains Chris Bilheimer. "In turn, I would receive 11 different mix CDs from people I had never met." Bilheimer also had to design the packaging for his mix CD. "I wanted to capture the fun and ridiculous nature of the music I chose for the mix, so I thought it would be fun to use the art of the disc itself as part of the cover. The main image is an illustration I did for the Sarah Silverman CD *Jesus Is Magic* of her riding a unicorn on a rainbow farting magic stars, and the blue sky is a sheet containing liner notes explaining the reason each song was included on the mix." Working within a tight budget, Bilheimer only used materials that he had in his office, printing everything with an inkjet printer. Avant Garde and Pump Triline are the typefaces used.

Product: CD
Client: Initiated by a friend
Artist: Various
Design: Chris Bilheimer
Country: USA

Hochschule für Gestaltung und Kunst Luzern—2007

This DVD showcases 130 minutes of moving images and audio works, which were produced at the Hochschule für Gestaltung und Kunst Luzern (University of Art and Design Lucerne). Cybu Richli and Fabienne Burri designed the package and interface for the DVD. They packaged the DVD in gray carton stock and applied all text and imagery using silk-screen printing to reflect the creative and experimental nature of the work on the DVD. Foundry Wilson typeface was used throughout.

Product: DVD
Client: University of Art and Design Lucerne
Design: Cybu Richli/Fabienne Burri
Country: Switzerland

Ragged Rubble

"This album features louder, noisier, and more politically charged songs than the band's previous releases," explains designer Bruce Willen. "Reflecting these changes, together with the drummer's love of maps, we created a shattered compostion by rearranging America's 50 states. We continued the abrasive color scheme onto the back cover where the band name is drawn as if each letter were a state, and the orange and purple color combination is also a nod to Baltimore City." As well as a CD version of the release, silk-screened LPs were also produced in a limited-edition run of 300 on clear vinyl.

Product: CD/Vinyl
Client/Label: Stationary (Heart)
Artist: Double Dagger
Design: Post Typography
Country: USA

X Marks the Spot

Andreas Emenius created the packaging for this compilation album with the brief to produce something special without standing out too much. "The idea for the design was to illustrate a booklet inspired by the music on the album," explains Emenius. "We chose to use people in abstract positions hinting at dancing or just at moving in general in a slightly surrealistic universe." Emenius commissioned Helle Mardahl to create the illustrations. To keep the rest of the information that had to appear on the package separate, the text has been placed on a sticker and then applied to the package. For the CD version, a white opaque jewel case has been used with a sticker applied to the front.

Product: CD/Vinyl
Client/Label: Route 33
Artist: Various
Design: Andreas Emenius
Illustration: Andreas Emenius with Helle Mardahl
Country: Sweden

Materials

Ooompa Zoompa/Evelyn

Neil Burrell created this 7in cover and its
illustrations using felt-tip pens, pencil, and
crayons on paper. "I wanted to illustrate the
cover with imagery that was warm, bright, and
full of cheer," he explains. "I wanted to 'sing the
song with my eyes' while holding a pen. Also
I like to scribble my own type and so have
done this too." The result is a bright, bold cover
featuring some unique and unusual illustrations.
The release was produced in a limited run on
a tactile, uncoated board stock.

Product: Vinyl
Client/Label: Akoustik Anarkhy Recordings
Artist: Neil Burrell
Design/Illustration: Frying Pan
Country: UK

The Clock

This DVD promo package was produced in a limited run of 500, with each package made from recycled DVD cases and used carrier bags. "The idea came from the concept for the video," explains Luke Taylor from design company us. "In turn the concept reflected the lyrics of the track, which talk about our overconsumption as a society and our ignorance about this. As producing a new DVD package would have been contradicting the message of the promo, we decided to create packaging with recycled items instead." The package also has minimal typography to keep the message clear and simple. The type was screen printed onto the package and set in Andale Mono.

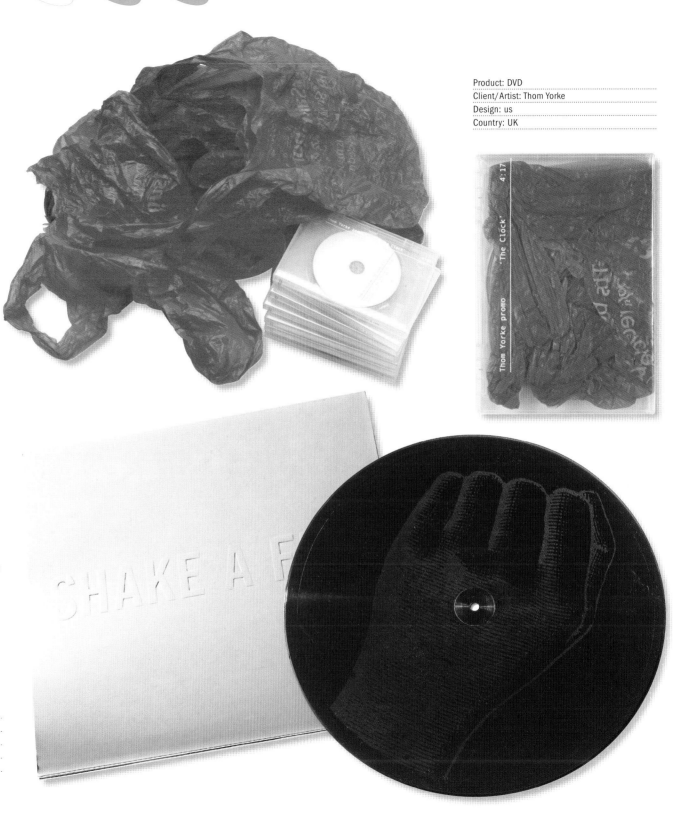

Product: DVD
Client/Artist: Thom Yorke
Design: us
Country: UK

Shake a Fist

Darren Wall designed this 12in cover with the brief for something with high production values in a small quantity, so he used an embossed typographic design on silver foil-covered stock. In addition, an illustration of a fist was etched into the b-side of the actual vinyl. "The great thing about doing this cover was that we were given permission to not use any copy except the band name and title on the cover—usually we have lots of credits and catalog numbers to put on the spine and back," explains Wall. "It means that the whole package is sparse and clean, which makes it quite an unusual record cover."

Product: Vinyl
Client/Label: EMI
Artist: Hot Chip
Design: Wallzo
Country: UK

The Chop

Non-Format designed the packaging for this EP featuring the music of The Chap, Hot Chip, Pier Bucci, Vincent Oliver, and Zilla. The vinyl has been packaged in a translucent antistatic bag with the LoEB logo printed on it in yellow ink; it follows the theme of each release on the label with the package designed to a template. To differentiate the releases the label is printed in a different color each time. Futura typeface has been used for the main text, while the logo has been custom made.

THE CHOP
THE CHAP
HOT CHIP
PIER BUCCI
VINCENT OLIVER
ZILLA

Product: Vinyl
Client/Label: LoEB/Lo Recordings
Artist: Various
Design: Non-Format
Countries: UK/USA

Form

Get Shot

Marc Antosch created this EP packaging.
"Because the budget was limited, the task
was to come up with a simple, but special
idea," Antosch explains. "I came up with this
1960s-style artwork, which in my opinion fitted
perfectly to the band's sound. Because I was
working a lot with screen printing at that time,
I printed the artwork directly on the protection
foil instead of the regular sleeve." Photography
featured on the album was shot exclusively for
this project, and ITC Avant Garde (Medium and
Bold) typeface has been used throughout this
promotional piece.

Product: Vinyl
Client/Artist: Frank Stallone & The Astronauts
Design: Tilt Design Studio
Photography: Markus Steffen
Country: Germany

Prayer for the Weekend/
The Worrying Kind

Ricky Tillblad designed this special-edition album cover as well as the packaging for the single *The Worrying Kind*. As he explains, most of the work he does for The Ark is inspired by the Art Deco and Art Nouveau design periods, and this album and single are no exception. Inspiration has been taken from old Art Deco posters and perfume packages in particular. "The singer in this band is, as I am, a huge fan of Art Deco design," explains Tillblad, "so the inspiration for the cover came from graphics from that era. I tried to find something in common between contemporary pop music and Art Deco." The logotype features a custom-made typeface, and the rest of the text on the cover is set in Mostra. The album is packaged in a JakeBox (Swedish card-based packaging). The cover has been printed four-color with silver foil blocking used for some of the graphic details. The single sleeve has been printed using one Pantone color together with gold foil. A leather-like paper has been used as it makes the foil crack, giving the package a vintage feel.

Product: CD
Client/Label: Roxy Recordings
Artist: The Ark
Design: Zion Graphics
Country: Sweden

PRAYER
FOR THE
WEEKEND

THE ARK

1 PRAYER FOR THE WEEKEND 4:22
2 THE WORRYING KIND 2:54
3 ABSOLUTELY NO DECORUM 3:45
4 LITTLE DYSFUNK YOU 4:07
5 NEW POLLUTION 4:30
6 THORAZINE CORAZON 3:42
7 PATHOLOGIZE 3:52
8 DEATH TO THE MARTYRS 3:52
9 ALL I WANT IS YOU 2:54
10 GIMME LOVE TO GIVE 3:57
11 URIEL 3:40

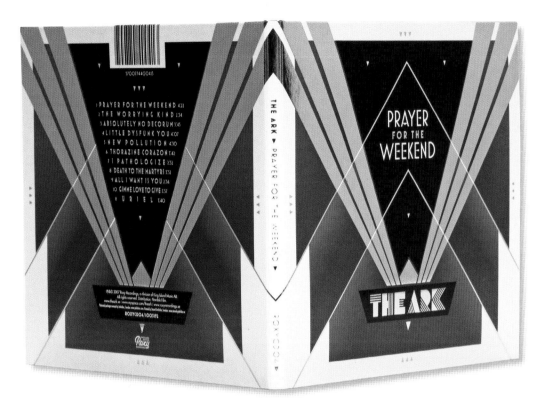

THE
WORRYIN
KIND

Product: CD
Client/Label: Roxy Recordings
Artist: The Ark
Design: Zion Graphics
Country: Sweden

Interaction

Well Deep: Ten Years of Big Dada Recordings

On a fairly tight budget, Oscar Bauer and Ewan Robertson created something a little different from the standard packaging for this special and celebratory release (double CD and DVD, including interviews and music videos). "With any compilation it's quite hard as you have to sum up all the past releases, which there may be no common theme for, so we aimed to show the past in a context which united them," explains Bauer. "We decided we'd collect all the released records and promotional material by the label from the past 10 years and place it in a museum context," he adds. "It is a tongue-in-cheek idea of making the records like artifacts." Johnston typeface, the London Underground font, was used as Big Dada releases underground music. This limited edition of the package has a spot gloss on the glass of the box in the photo. "We felt the picture alone may have looked a little old, so we applied the gloss to make it more contemporary," explains Bauer.

Product: CD/DVD
Client/Label: Big Dada Recordings
Artist: Various
Design: Oscar Bauer/Ewan Robertson
Photography: James Musgrave
Country: UK

The Looks

"The record label directed us with our design propositions to how much crazier we could go in terms of concept; since we had a big budget, we had a lot of leeway," explains designer Yannick Desranleau. "So it was pretty much 'do whatever you want' from that point." However, Seripop kept the front cover minimal to reflect the house/techno contained within and follow the band's request ("be as white as possible"). "To go around this constraint and play off a sort of minimum/maximum type of paradox within the design, we wrote the band's name and album title in a lettering made of a succession of tiny lines, and the words took all the available space on the cover," adds Desranleau. The lettering has been overprinted in spot silver on the collage at the bottom of the cover. "Our concept was a simple pun on the record title. The front cover has a woman with her eyes cut out. The eyes are die-cut and allow the psychedelic patterns on the inner sleeve to show. The inner sleeve can be turned to create different views or ways of looking," he adds.

Product: CD/Vinyl
Client/Label: Last Gang Records/Universal
Artist: MSTRKRFT
Design: Seripop
Country: Canada

Form

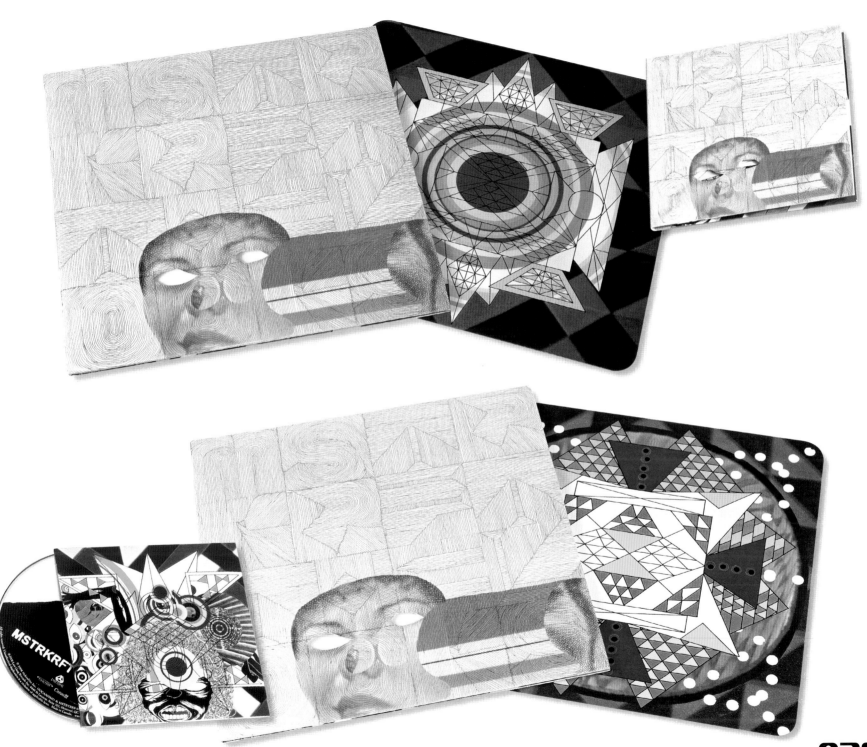

I Love Trouble

Brad Kayal designed the package for this debut EP CD with the brief for it to make a good first impression. "For quite a while I've found the slide rule to be really aesthetically interesting," explains Kayal. "This, combined with a band called The Information, seemed like a good starting point." Kayal created imagery that is a series of made-up fields and data sets to make the whole analog calculator seem horribly complex. However, if the user rotates the actual disc to "EP" on the open end, the "result" field will show "The Information." "I created most of it in Illustrator and then beat it up through a series of photocopies to make the final printing feel more vintage," adds Kayal. All of the type is basic Courier, chosen as it relates to older-style printouts and computers. While the CD itself is fairly straightforward, with a three-color printing process, the more elaborate packaging required a custom die-cut and was printed on a special uncoated French paper.

Product: CD
Client/Artist: The Information
Design: Brad Kayal
Country: USA

Standing in the Way of Control

David Lane produced branded packaging for the promo and remixed versions of this single. He designed custom-printed packaging tape, which was used to seal and brand all the formats (except the CD and follow-on runs). To open the record sleeves, the tape had to be cut—thus the owner had to destroy the product to access the music. The imagery was taken from the video and rephotographed from an analog monitor. "The tape could be viewed as standing in the way of control or as the control," explains Lane. He designed a custom title type for the single and its promotional material, and set the label copy and credits in Amasis.

Product: CD/Vinyl
Client/Label: Back Yard Recordings
Artist: Gossip
Design: David Lane
Country: UK

Ornamental Etherworld

Jeff Harrison created this CD packaging, the concept for which came directly from the band. The CD unfolds and refolds to create a dolls' house. It is complete with detailed interiors and a fold-in roof, which were made in miniature and photographed. The CD itself is the feature shag carpet rug with pop-out characters based directly on the band members' style, down to the handmade clothing that the band actually wears at gigs. The handmade sets and props include a tiny sausage and eggs on the stove. Galaxie Polaris typeface was used for its delicate nature. A limited-edition of 500 were printed, die-cut, and sold through the band's website and at gigs.

Product: CD
Client/Artist: Vonnegut Dollhouse
Art Direction: Ian Grais/Rethink Communications
Design: Rethink Communications
Photography: Clinton Hussey
Country: Canada

Alternate Ending 1: The Glimmering Noise

This DVD is an insider's look at the problems facing current architectural practice. Initially Michael Meredith, together with WeWorkForThem, was only going to have a printed manifesto (*Notes for those beginning the discipline of architecture*), but then decided to make this accompanying DVD. WeWorkForThem designed the package. "We made the artwork based on the idea of glimmering noise and how that looked," explains Michael Cina. The manifesto is also printed on a poster included with the DVD. The package was specially made with a die-cut to hold the DVD. Didot typeface was used throughout.

Product: DVD
Client: YouWorkForThem
Artist: Michael Meredith
Design: WeWorkForThem
Country: USA

Battery Milk

Maiko Kuzunishi designed this limited-edition
CD package, which was letterpress printed.
"For the band's poster artwork, Peregrine Honig
had drawn an image of a woman with an afro
squeezing her breasts to form letters with her
milk," explains Kuzunishi. "Dillon loved the
image and wanted to use it for the cover of the
album too... and it was completely appropriate
for the album title, *Battery Milk*." To reflect the
dynamic, energetic nature of the music, Kuzunishi
has drawn bold flower imagery that features
both on the cover and inside the album package.
Hand-drawn typefaces have been used for the
album title and band name, and Rodeo Crown
Fill has been used for all other text.

Product: CD
Client: Royal Artist Group
Artist: Mike Dillon's Go-Go Jungle
Label: Hyena Records
Design: Decoylab
Illustration: Peregrine Honig
Country: USA

On Radar: Vol 1

This compilation CD package features music from several new bands signed to the Radar label. Nick Griffiths' brief was to produce something that felt precious and beautiful, while staying within a limited budget. "The main focus was finding a way of combining both packaging and artwork so that they became one and the same, while providing the user with a tactile and interactive experience," explains Griffiths. "A folded poster on which the CD was attached felt like the natural solution as the client was keen on the idea of producing a collectible series." The package is made up of a natural, delicate recycled newsprint paper together with a glossy vinyl sticker used to seal each of the 3,500 copies. The dark woodland illustration has been created around the label's heart logo and screen printed onto the package. DIN typeface was used throughout.

Product: CD
Client/Label: Radar
Artist: Various
Design: Peppered Sprout
Country: UK

Interaction

B Heavy and Loaded
with Dynamite

Dimaquina created the packaging for this mix-tape by DJ Chico Dub, a Jamaican DJ based in Rio de Janeiro, for distribution to a selected group of artists and cultural producers. "The challenge was to create an extremely low-budget product that could still translate the creativity of its content," explains Antonio Pedro. "A tick sheet of offset paper printed on a black-and-white laser printer and manual interferences made with stencil masks made each package unique. When opened, the sleeve turns into a poster." The roughness and experimentalism of the music inspired Dimaquina. Helvetica Rounded has been used for most of the text, while the title type is based on Naiv-Fat. Dimaquina printed the black-and-white packaging in its studio, on a thick stock, then applied color by hand.

Product: CD
Client/Artist: DJ Chico Dub
Design: Dimaquina
Country: Brazil

Milky Disco

This album is a disco accompaniment to the Milky Globe album *Magic Waves.* Non-Format designed a package that would fit in with the rest of the Milky series of releases. "We wanted to create something typographic since the Milky Globe release, a 12in single, featured a typographic illustration by Deanne Cheuk," explains Forss. "We created a typeface specially for the project and then created abstract shapes to accompany the typography and to add depth and color." The supporting type is TYP1451B, and the CD is housed in a jewel case and slipcase.

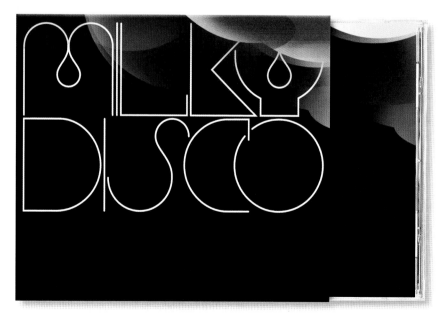

Product: CD
Client/Label: Lo Recordings
Artist: Various
Design: Non-Format
Illustration: Non-Format
Countries: UK/USA

Seven Stabs

For this CD cover, Matthew Bolger and Emelie Lidström used the digipak format, playing with the idea of overlaying transparent gloss vinyl stickers with a silk-screened image over illustration on a matte digipak cover. "By doing this we could create different textures and combinations of illustrations, placing the vinyl sticker by hand at different locations on the back of each cover," explains Bolger. The cover contains two vinyl stickers, one transparent sticker with a silk-screened image of graphic line illustration in yellow, and a black sticker (containing the band's name and album title) to seal the digipak shut. "'To open the cover and retrieve the CD, the listener has to cut or stab the sticker to unlock the cover. With this action of stabbing or slashing, we wanted to evoke the album title. The photographic imagery again relates directly to the album title. We felt that the first thing you want to do when you have a balloon is to fly it and second is to burst or stab it," adds Bolger. Folk Art typeface is used on the cover for its pixelated form.

Product: CD
Client/Label: Greyslate Records
Artist: The Redneck Manifesto
Design: M&E
Photography: Emelie Lidström
Country: Ireland

Bande à Part

Dylan Kendle designed this cover, creating a visual identity that was a development from Nouvelle Vague's first album (see page 122). "This had to link to the first album, but be a step forward," he explains. "It was the same principle; a clash of styles, hard modern typography with a twist offset against wistful illustrations of girls." Verhoeven created several images that have been used across all this album's releases, as shown here. A recut version of Futura Black was hand cut, stenciled, and used for titles, and Futura Book was used for track details. The print spec was quite high for a commercial album—all paper artwork was two spot colors, one fluorescent and black with a matte laminate and a spot gloss UV overprinted on the fluorescent. All card sleeves were printed black on the inside.

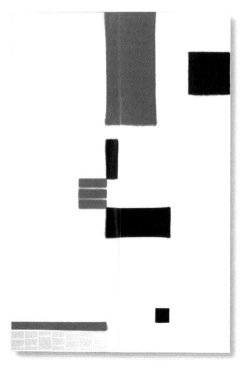

Product: CD/Vinyl
Client/Label: Peacefrog
Artist: Nouvelle Vague
Design/Art Direction: Dylan Kendle
Illustration: Julie Verhoeven
Country: UK

Interaction

Paper
manipulation

This is a Quiet Room

Craig Ward created the CD package for this album by the lo-fi, hugely eclectic, and vaguely psychedelic band Shiny Tight Stuff. "I've known the band a long time and I was entrusted with a virtual carte blanche for the design of the package, the only hindrance being the practically nonexistent budget," explains Ward. "Taking the name of the album and the nature of the band's music as starting points, I began sketching out ideas initially inspired by the psychedelic poster art of the 1970s," he adds. "The notion of quietness led me to eventually use the band's name to depict a person's face with their fingers to their lips, as if they were hushing someone. I wanted to reflect the lo-fi nature of the album, which was mostly home-produced bar some mastering, so I created a linocut illustration of the face and hand image, which I used to hand print the first 50 sleeves. The title of the album appears in the spine section of the case." This resulted in 50 unique versions of the album cover. Ward also created linocuts for the spine typography and the reverse of the cover.

Product: CD
Client/Artist: Shiny Tight Stuff
Label: Angel's Hairbrush
Design: Words Are Pictures
Country: UK

Copenhagen Jazz Festival

re-public created this CD package to reflect the new identity for the Copenhagen Jazz Festival and its promotional trip to the USA. "Copenhagen Jazz Festival has a design manual, so I had to create something new with the exciting graphics and typography," explains Romeo Vidner. "It's jazz music, so I had to improvise with the design to get the right expression. Because they have a very strict and simple identity, I chose to work with different varnish and emboss effects to make it look more playful and laid-back." Instead of printing the track list in color, he used a varnish to give the package a sophisticated look, with embossing on the front cover. The typeface used is DuNord, a custom-made font for the wider identity program.

Product: CD
Client: Copenhagen Jazz Festival
Design: re-public
Country: Denmark

Old Mayor

Owen Gildersleeve designed this CD packaging and accompanying promotional poster. "The band wanted a CD package and poster that were low-cost and easy to reproduce so they could hand them out to promoters, but at the same time were good enough to sell at their shows," he explains. "They have a very dark and heavy sound, and so in an attempt to represent this, I decided it would be good to use quite gritty, hand-drawn imagery with a limited color palette, printing black onto a mocha-colored stock. This also meant that the costs of creating the promo items would be fairly low." As the band has two members, the poster features a large tree split down the middle, with the roots coming together around the band's logo. For the front cover of the CD, Gildersleeve has hand drawn what appear to be large, abstract, textural shapes surrounding the band's logo and text, but on opening the CD the shapes form the band's initials. Gildersleeve used Garamond typeface because it reflected the subtleties of the music while still having a dark edge.

Paper manipulation

Product: CD
Client/Artist: Old Mayor
Design: Owen Gildersleeve
Country: UK

043

RGB

Jewboy designed the package for this DVD of Tushia's video works with the brief simply to listen to the music and do what he thought best for it. "It is a great way to work, but stressful," he explains. "In *RGB* the videos have a strong aggressive color which is impossible to ignore, so I deliberately chose to describe the content rather than to show it." The main idea for the cover design hinges on the use of rubber stamps to apply the title, *RGB*. "It is intended to distort and disrupt," explains Jewboy. "Once we got the covers back from the print house, we sat down and stamped each cover with the three different rubber stamps. I think that dissonance between human custom-made and machine production resembles Teder's manifesto of a sophisticated cold touch together with the human touch."

RGB / AN EXPERIMENTAL VIDEO PROJECT, DISINTEGRATES MOMENTS OF LIFE INTO FRACTALS OF TIME AND SPACE. RGB – RED, GREEN, AND BLUE – SIGNIFIES THE THREE COLORS OF LIGHT, WHICH CAN BE MIXED TO PRODUCE ANY OTHER COLOR. WESTERN CULTURE TRUSTS VISION, WHILE ITS IMAGES HAVE GROWN INTO GATHERINGS OF PIXEL-COLORED CELLS. RGB, AWARE OF THE MEDIUM, QUESTIONS THIS TRUST AND SIMULTANEOUSLY ATTEMPTS TO EXPAND THE BOUNDARIES OF THE ORDINARY VISUALS FOUND IN EVERYDAY LIFE. ITS IMAGES ARE ACCOMPANIED BY EXPERIMENTAL AUDIO AMBIANCE AND MINIMAL BEATS. RGB TAKES THE VIEWER THROUGH A SLOW, HYPNOTIC JOURNEY INTO "PIXEL", COLORED "REALITY".
VIDEOS BY GAL TUSHIA / MUSIC BY GAL TUSHIA AND DAVID OVADIA   2005/TEDERMUSIC ALL RIGHTS RESERVED
WWW.TEDERMUSIC.COM

DESIGN: JEWBOY CORPORATION™ / WWW.JEWBOY.CO.IL

RGB · EXPERIMENTAL VIDEO WORKS / GAL TUSHIA // TDR007 DVD

TDR007 RGB /
EXPERIMENTAL VIDEOS
GAL TUSHIA

DVD

Product: DVD
Client/Label: Teder Music
Artist: Gal Tushia
Design: Jewboy Corporation™
Country: Israel

DOT

"The music on *DOT* has a strong feeling of the ever evolving, yet monotonous," explains Jewboy, "as if 'patterns' are constantly growing, so with the design of the package I wanted to translate this feeling." He has achieved this by overprinting an image of a tree with a series of dots on the cover to give the idea of something evolving and growing beyond what would actually be physically possible. "I made a dot, scanned it, enlarged it, then added grays into the pattern," he explains. "I did this three times to create three rubber stamps which when stamped on each other create random new patterns of the same style." Each cover was printed using one Pantone color and then the three rubber stamps.

Product: CD
Client/Label: Teder Music
Artist: Ziv Jacob
Design: Jewboy Corporation™
Country: Israel

Paper manipulation

DMmPPPs^^{

Jewboy designed the CD cover for this release. "This is not an easy listening CD," he explains. "The computer has gone mad here… in normal life computers distort sounds or images, but on this cover the image of a computer gets distorted to the point that it becomes a series of random shapes." The cover has a mixture of digital and handmade imagery. "I tried to keep the imagery just on the border of abstract," adds Jewboy. As with many of the Teder Music releases, this lo-fi design uses rubber stamps to apply the imagery and text, making each cover unique.

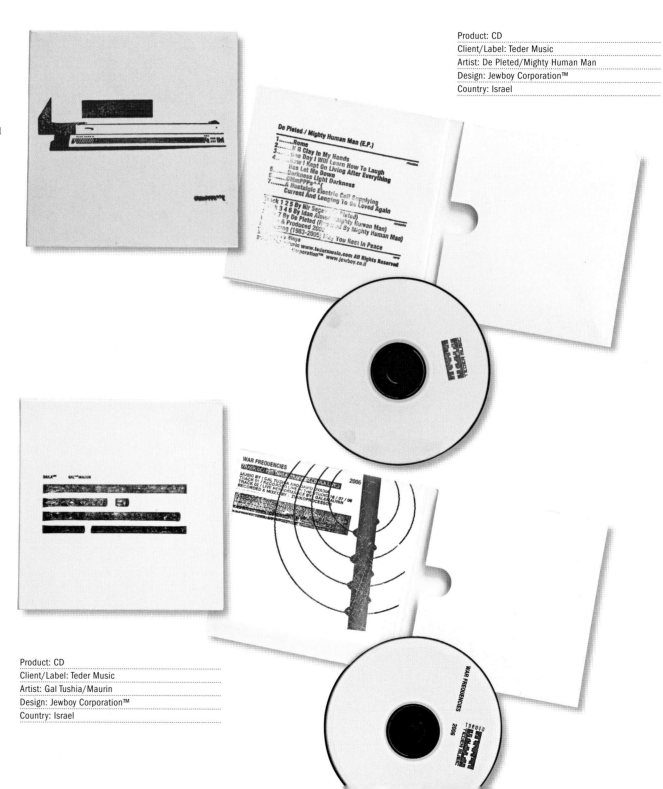

Product: CD
Client/Label: Teder Music
Artist: De Pleted/Mighty Human Man
Design: Jewboy Corporation™
Country: Israel

Daila Live

"The music on this CD was recorded live at a club in Jerusalem while the Lebanon/Israel war was pounding at both sides," explains Jewboy. Roughly translated, the title *Daila* means "enough (to) the." "The meaning is clear; enough to the war, corruption, pollution, and so on," adds Jewboy. "To translate this idea onto the cover, I created a rubber-stamp image that can be translated as sound levels or censorship, and I tried as much as I could to make it fit the political background we were experiencing at that time."

Product: CD
Client/Label: Teder Music
Artist: Gal Tushia/Maurin
Design: Jewboy Corporation™
Country: Israel

The Warning

Darren Wall designed this 12in cover. The blocks on the cover were developed as a visual metaphor for the music—they are wooden blocks with plastic wedges forced into them. "I think they look friendly, but there's a tension there as well which is present in the music," explains Wall. "On the 12in version we 'hid' all the colorful blocks inside on the gatefold and debossed the linework onto the outer sleeve. It's like an in-joke for people familiar with the CD packaging as that is colorful and bold on the outside and sparse and black and white on the inside—the reverse of the 12in."

Product: Vinyl
Client/Label: EMI
Artist: Hot Chip
Design: Wallzo
Country: UK

Paper manipulation

047

Same Man Vol. 1

"I wanted to design a cover that was eye-catching and colorful, and that had a disco feeling," Ricky Tillblad explains. "I came up with the idea to use this strong image of an eye together with striking colorful shapes." The result is a powerful cover with strong imagery and elegant use of type. Tillblad has used Chalet typeface and then stretched some parts of the lettering to create the long lines that run over the image. The cover image has been printed in CMYK together with foil blocking for the letters, creating a cover with a seductive feel.

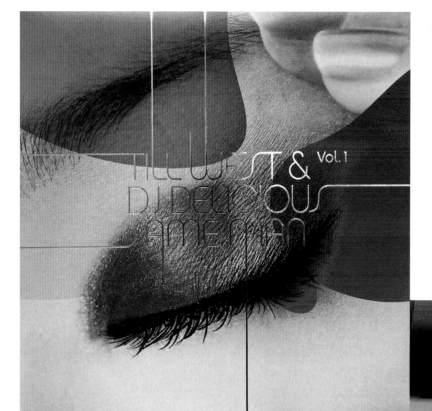

Product: Vinyl
Client/Label: Refune
Artist: Till West & DJ Delicious
Design: Zion Graphics
Country: Sweden

Dance series

For this series of 12in dance music vinyls,
Tillblad created a sleeve that could be used
in various ways for several different releases,
together with new stickers and labels. The
shape of the Size logo, which he also designed,
inspired the cover design. The logo has been
partly silver foiled and partly die-cut to make
the different-colored labels on the vinyl inside
visible through the cover. The labels and stickers
have been printed in Pantone silver and various
Pantone colors. The cover typeface is Foundry
Form Sans, chosen for its industrial feel.

Product: Vinyl
Client/Label: Size Records
Artist: Various
Design: Zion Graphics
Country: Sweden

Mary-Anne Hobbs Warrior Dubz

David Bray created the artwork for this
compilation album, curated by Mary-Anne
Hobbs, a DJ on the UK's Radio 1. The featured
artists include Milanese, Burial, Kode9, and
Benga. The CD version of the release has a six-
page roll-fold insert to accommodate the full
composition of Bray's illustration, showing all
three girls. A slipcase over the jewel case makes
the whole package tactile and offers a sense of
elegance. The LP version has been spread across
three pieces of vinyl and housed in a full gatefold
sleeve to give impact to Bray's illustrations.

Product: CD/Vinyl
Client/Label: Planet Mu Records
Artist: Various
Design/Illustration: David Bray
Artwork: Ben Curzon
Country: UK

MNTrL typeface

The MNTrL CD package shown here contains all font files for the MNTrL typeface, as well as printable type sample sheets that showcase it. MNTrL was created to replace the mechanical flip-letterforms used by Montreal's transport system. The cover artwork features the singular element used in the construction of the modular letterforms. The booklet showcases the stylistic elements of the typeface in comparison to other modular typefaces and also features rejected letterforms that were not incorporated in the final font. The printed inserts also feature hand-applied postproduction details such as font metrics and perforated guidelines that indicate coarse modular element guidelines.

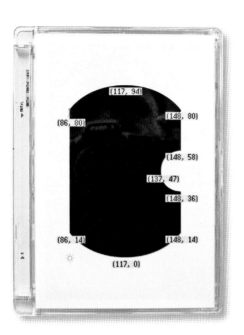
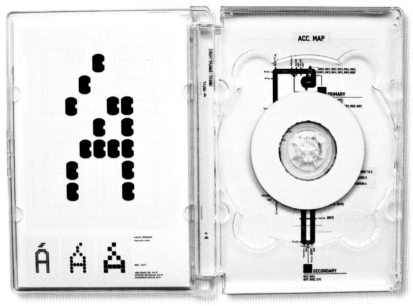

Product: CD
Client: ±
Design: ± (Peter Crnokrak)
Country: Canada

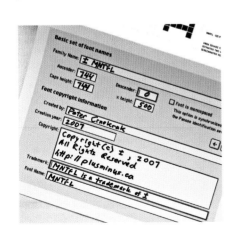

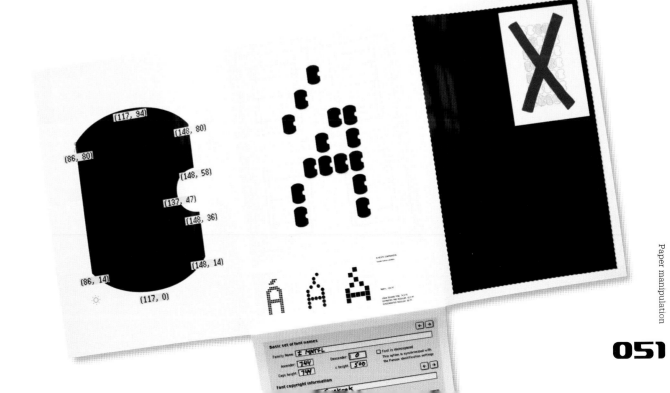

Grace Kelly/Relax

Shown here are two singles by Mika. These sleeves are a continuation of the bright, colorful visual world created for Mika by design studio Airside, artist Da Wack (Mika's sister), and Mika himself. The titles of both singles have been die-cut into brown card sleeves to reveal the inner-sleeve illustrations. Airside developed Mika's logo and created the hand-drawn fonts specifically for his releases.

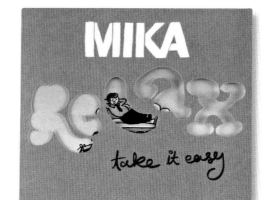

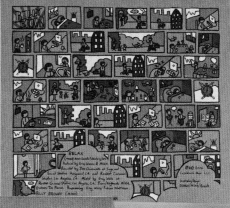

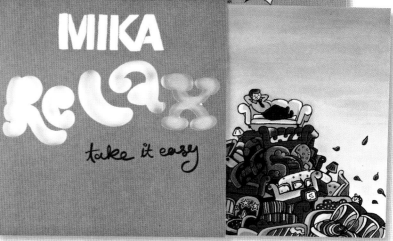

Product: Vinyl
Client/Label: Universal/Casablanca
Artist: Mika
Design: Airside/Da Wack/Mika
Country: UK

The Sacred Harp Library

Pete Hellicar designed these sleeves with the idea of a library collection look in mind. He created a generic sleeve design that could be customized with different-colored labels on the records themselves to identify them. "We were inspired by the Folkways sleeves and some of the work of Will Bankhead for the Honest Jon's label," explains Hellicar. "We based the main cover image on a symbol of plenty from a book of occult symbols. This seemed to fit with the whole image that they wanted to portray." Hellicar has used Warnock Pro typeface in various weights on the limited release. The sleeve itself has been created using uncoated card and features a blind deboss for the logotype, silk-screened graphics, and a die-cut center hole. Each process was used to add to the feeling of handicraft.

Product: Vinyl
Client/Label: Memphis Industries
Artist: The Sacred Harp Library
Design: Pete Hellicar
Country: UK

Paper manipulation

053

Granite

Paul West and Kate Payne designed the package for this single release. A mazelike graphic image was created for use on the cover and applied using a spot varnish. The inner sleeve of the double pouch casing has been given a reflective black finish with a matte gray finish to the outer sleeve. Albertus typeface was chosen for use throughout the package.

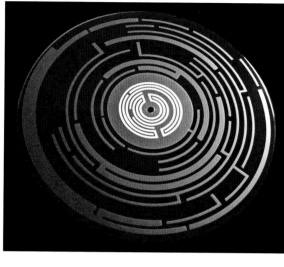

Product: CD
Client/Label: Warner Music Ltd.
Artist: Pendulum
Design: Form
Country: UK

Life's Addictions

Laura Snell and Jess Bonham designed this debut album packaging. "We were given almost complete freedom to respond to the music in whichever way we wanted," explains Snell. "The only requirement was that the packaging had to be modern and unique, as well as practical and stylish. Because it was only a small run, we were able to be experimental with processes and the format." The idea was to create a package that was playful and sexy on the inside, and simple and stylish on the outside. "We wanted the outer sleeve to partially conceal the imagery on the inside so that it is a bit of a visual tease," she adds. "We decided on a high-gloss black sleeve with embossed lettering as it offered a supermodern and tactile feel." In addition, the package includes a poster, which has some elements applied using a high-gloss screen-printed varnish, in contrast to the matte paper. An extra pocket has been created within the package that holds the poster.

Product: CD
Client/Artist: Shiva Park
Design: Laura Snell/Jess Bonham
Country: UK

Paper manipulation

Klima

When Richard Robinson created this cover, he worked closely with one of Klima's members on the design. "I had been working on a new typeface and had heard an early demo of the Klima album and thought it was perfect for this artist," he explains. "I approached the label and discussed the initial typeface and they agreed. I had several conversations with Angèle from Klima about how to incorporate some photos she had. The solution was to treat the images and use the type as a window." Robinson wanted to show clearly the delicate beauty of the record without being too whimsical, so the hard edges of the type combined with the textured images works well. With this, he used each part of the package to its maximum potential, creating a free-flowing typographic treatment for all the secondary copy. The booklet is 12-page roll-fold printed on a matte stock with a satin seal. This was then spot varnished with the logo to highlight the typography.

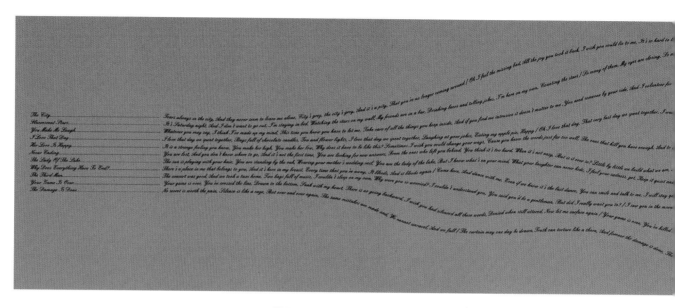

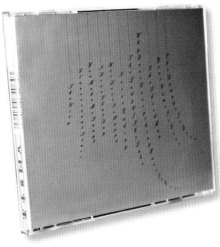

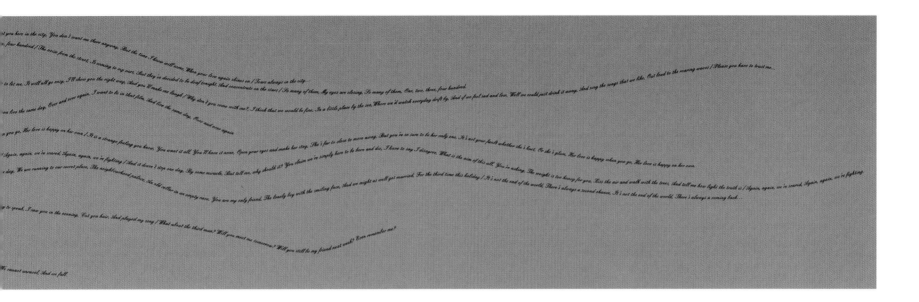

Product: CD
Client/Label: Peacefrog
Artist: Klima
Design: Richard Robinson
Photography: Nicolas Toutain
Country: UK

Paper manipulation

Patrick Duffy
No Days Off
UK

When designing packages for CDs, vinyl, or DVDs, what inspires you?
It's partly the music, partly the artist, and partly my own desire to create something interesting. Sometimes it's necessary to faithfully represent the artist and their music through the design; other times, it's more effective to run counter to expectations and create something that stands apart from the music, something that will create interest by itself and not necessarily illustrate what's contained within the packaging.

What do you most enjoy about working on such design projects?
I like the challenge of having to interpret a brand new piece of music; sometimes the artwork will be a person's first point of contact with the music, so it's got to be right. I also like the idea that what you do is at least semipermanent— someone could pick it up in a secondhand record store in 30 years' time if such things still exist.

What is the most important function for a cover/package to perform?
Ultimately, the function of the cover is to sell the product, as XTC's *Go 2* by Hipgnosis showed. To my mind, the greatest achievement is to create something beautiful which stands the test of time; in that context, The Beatles' *The White Album* by Richard Hamilton and Joy Division's *Unknown Pleasures* by Peter Saville are two that I would say are beyond successful. I can't imagine anyone not being captivated by them, now or in the future.

What is the most interesting piece of packaging you have come across in this area?
Add N to (X)'s *Little Black Rocks in the Sun* is one record that I remember buying purely for the packaging: a 10in hexagonal record housed in a black sleeve that unfolds like a flower. Simple, and perfectly matches the music.

What is your favorite vinyl package of all time?
Other than the examples I mentioned earlier, probably *Metal Box* by PiL. Again, the packaging perfectly matches the music, right down to the difficulty of actually getting the records out to play. It brings to mind those canisters that governments periodically bury or shoot out into space filled with "relevant" music; if anything deserves to be preserved for the enlightenment of future generations (or Martians), this is it.

What do you think the future holds for music and movie packaging now that so much music (and soon movies) can be downloaded, and how do you think the role of the graphic designer might change because of this?
I think that the death knell of physical packaging has been sounded far too early and that, rather than an either/or situation, we will eventually settle into a world where the physical and the digital will exist side by side. Just as certain types of people will always prefer the ease of downloading, others will prefer to exchange their cash for a physical item. I don't see this changing anytime soon, so the role of the designer is simply to adapt and get used to solving the same problem in a different way.

What can designers do to move with the "digital times" and offer buyers something other than simply a thumbnail image of an album cover when they download music?
When considering an album, either as a designer or a consumer, the cover is only part of the story; a lot of the fun and interest also comes from the booklets, inserts, and even the disc itself sometimes. This is often what gets lost when downloading, but there's no reason that these extras can't be replaced with digital counterparts: little animations instead of booklets, audio or video of someone reading lyrics to you, printable stickers or transfers.

Matt Dixon
EMI Records
UK

What is the most important function for a cover/package to perform?
To reflect the personality of the artist and the nature of the music. In 2007 I was fortunate enough to work on two of the best albums, which, in my humble opinion, also had two of the best campaigns—LCD Soundsystem and Róisín Murphy. Both were very different, yet made by amazing artists with strong personalities. I believe the artwork (and photos, videos, etc.) in both cases fully translated how great both pieces of music are.

What is the most interesting piece of packaging you have come across in this area?
Almost anything by Pizzicato Five was amazing. If you ever see the book about their artwork and packaging with the whole of their career before your eyes, you can't fail to be impressed. They never let me down.

How do you approach the briefing of designers?
Mostly by having the artist work as closely as possible with them. Most of the time, an artist either knows their designer or knows who they want to use. My job is just to make sure all goes to plan and advise when I need to, if everything's going to plan. On the odd occasion that I need to brief a designer, I try to get a few of them to pitch, having given them some music to listen to and told them roughly what direction the artist wants to take. Then I get a couple to meet the artist and see who clicks.

Are decisions about covers/packages based on their marketability or their design aesthetic?
I'd say the design, but in an ideal world both go hand in hand. A couple of years ago I worked with Hot Chip on *The Warning* album campaign, which totally worked on both counts.

What do you think the future holds for music and movie packaging now that so much music (and soon movies) can be downloaded, and how do you think the role of the graphic designer might change because of this?
Two things—we need to put more into how download packages are put together, and for those buying the physical product, we need to make it look like something you would want to own again. The recent Radiohead album worked amazingly on both fronts. The box set is really beautiful.

What can designers do to move with the "digital times" and offer buyers something other than simply a thumbnail image of an album cover when they download music?
Keep pushing the boundaries, but the boundaries are marked by digital retailers. There's only so much they "allow" at the moment so there's only so much you can do. It's not like working with physical releases at all. Also you have to take into account what iPods/Zunes/etc. are capable of playing/doing.

Content

02

In this chapter, different artwork and typographic solutions within the design of CD, DVD, and vinyl packaging are explored. From photography to the use of mixed media and illustration, the artwork and typographic solutions shown in this chapter give a great global snapshot of a broad range of striking visual design.

In the examples shown on the following pages, gone are the days of the artist's name and headshot on an album cover. Instead, designers are working with photographers or illustrators to create innovative imagery, or are using typography to its full potential to create outstanding type-only packaging solutions.

From the outrageous to the sublime, as long as the package artwork and typography provide a voice for the content within, the design has done its job.

Artwork

Lounge.Co

In creating the cover for this compilation of Colombian electronic music, curated by Mélodie Lounge, Cuartopiso visually recreated the DIY aesthetic of the music on the CD. "We wanted to create something homemade using domestic resources, but something that was also clearly manipulated in the computer," explains Alejandro Posada. "We digitally photographed small dioramas, which we created with cut-out hand-drawn images and green thread, and then combined these images with vector graphics and type." The hand-drawn logo was combined with the simple and classic Akzidenz (Mélodie Lounge's identity font) and the more contemporary Envy typeface. The result is a charming lo-fi cover with a handmade feel.

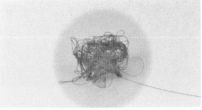

Product: CD
Label/Client: Mélodie Lounge Musique
Design: Cuartopiso
Photography: Diana Montoya
Country: Colombia

Islands of Memory

Islands of Memory features the found recordings of some old material by Alog. Grandpeople designed its cover and packaging, creating some quite abstract visuals for it. The imagery is a continuation from Alog's previous compilation (*Catch That Totem!*) record cover, which Grandpeople also designed; its artwork was inspired by Japanese manga. Since both albums share the same type of content (old material), Grandpeople reflected this by connecting them visually.

Product: Vinyl
Client/Label: Creaked Records
Artist: Alog
Design: Grandpeople
Countries: Norway/Switzerland

Brakhage

Meland and Marhaug played live music to the movie screenings of legendary moviemaker Stan Brakhage, hence the title *Brakhage*. With the originally silent movies having content like autopsies, the artwork moved along dark, neo-psychedelic pathways. Listening to the music without the movies, its connection to them is lost. The function of the visuals was to fill in the gaps for listeners without a knowledge of Brakhage's visual universe.

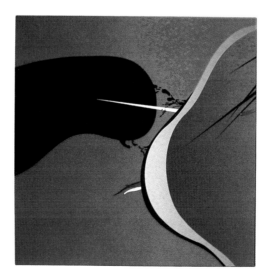

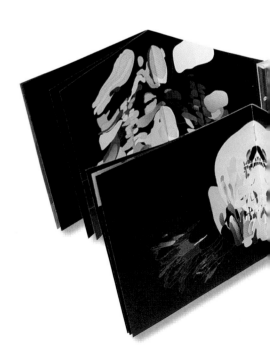

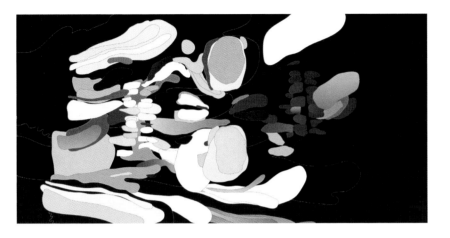

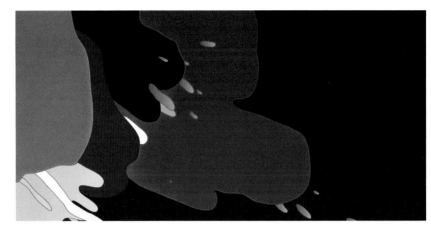

Product: Vinyl
Client/Label: Melektronikk
Artist: Andreas Meland/Lasse Marhaug
Design: Grandpeople
Country: Norway

For the People, By the People/ What it Is & What it Ain't/ Mind Trip

Each EP in this collection features a different artist. Jon Burgerman created the packaging with the brief to keep certain elements the same across the sleeves and record labels, such as the winding road, but create a new character and color scheme for each one. "The idea was to give each release its own distinct personality, relating to the musician on the record where possible," he explains. "But also to build up a collection of characters across all the EPs." Hand-rendered type has been used throughout the sleeves to give a more handmade feel as well as to tie in with the character illustration style.

Product: Vinyl
Client/Label: Winding Road Records
Artist: Various
Design: Jon Burgerman.com
Illustration: Jon Burgerman.com
Country: UK

Some Thing Came Up/Boy Bitten, Blood On The Moon/ Yes Yes Y'all

Oliver Walker designed the package for the release of this album and its subsequent singles by Mekon (John Gosling), who collaborated with Bobby Gillespie, Roxanne Shante, Alan Vega, Marc Almond, Rita Brown, Afrika Bambaataa, and Kev Pill Mob. "The final package for the CD and singles was designed to create a classical environment for the photograph used, the artists, and the music," explains Walker. "Because the pure photo could not be visible on the outside of the packaging for legal reasons, special thought had to be put into how best to display this image." As a result, there is no printed material inside the jewel case, leaving a clear pack within an "O" card sleeve with all the text on its back. The photo was printed onto the disc. "In this way we produced a very simple package, which displayed the photo in its purest form. As you slide off the 'O' card, you are presented with the McQueen photo, which you then have to push your thumb into the middle of to release the CD," adds Walker. Typeface Caslon Old Face was used throughout. A gold foil on the album cover adds to its classical feel.

Product: CD
Client/Label: Pias/Wall Of Sound
Artist: Mekon (John Gosling)
Art Direction: Alexander McQueen/Oliver Walker
Design: Ollystudio
Photography: Gregorio Pagliaro/Nathan Seabrook
Country: UK

Clip & Glide

Pandarosa created this CD package. Its size and design is based on a previous package design that Pandarosa created specifically for this label. "When we heard the title—*Clip and Glide*—we instantly got the imagery of eagles/birds of prey gliding high in the clouds in our heads from the 'Glide' element in the title," explains Ariel Aguilera. "For this element we created various wind- and cloud-like forms which these birds were part of, and to address the 'Clip' element of the title we wanted to break these organic forms with a geometric, more rigid form which cut right through the middle of it, almost like thunder and lightning coming from the clouds. Obviously, hearing the music featured in the CD also helped and related very well with the visuals, as it was extremely organic and ambient while still being electronic in nature." The imagery used on the package came from Pandarosa's image library.

Product: CD
Client/Label: AKA Ltd.
Artist: Distruc
Design: Pandarosa
Countries: Australia/Japan

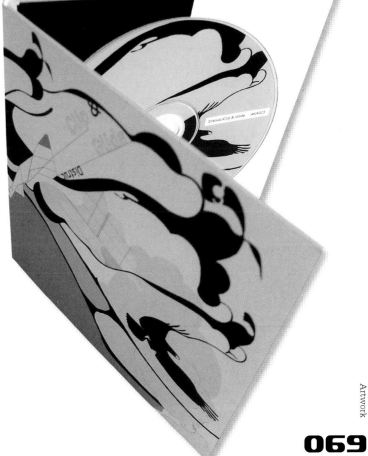

Artwork

Sun + Void

Qian Qian created a collage for this cover based on The Current Group's visual works including drawing, photography, and design. "I think this idea matches the way the band does music: a collective effort," explains Qian. "So I asked all the members of the band to give whatever they wanted to contribute to the cover art, then I did my selection, manipulation, and composition of all the imagery." The circle motif that features throughout the package relates to the album title *Sun + Void*. Qian has opted for a minimal type treatment using Temple Gothic on the front and back covers. Made as a limited edition of 50, the CD was sold online and at live shows.

THE CURRENT GROUP SUN + VOID

Product: CD
Client/Artist: The Current Group
Design: Qian Qian
Photography: Di Wu
Cover Art Contribution: Jonathan James/Nathan Cook/Steven Kramer/Qian Qian
Country: USA

Sludge Test

Another Limited Rebellion created this album cover, representing the balance between the beauty and aggression that is evoked by Gutbucket's avant-garde punk-jazz music. The band wanted the image of the girl with a knife, which had been created for them previously, to be the centerpiece of the album. "The girl captures the simultaneous sweetness and aggression of their music succinctly, so the package was designed to complement this by utilizing the innocent bright pink throughout as a contrast to the girl's knife and literal bucket of guts," explains Noah Scalin. "Since it was decided that the package would include a slip-cover, the booklet provided an opportunity to expand on the concept. The faux newspaper clipping hints that there is more to the story of the girl and implies a gritty reality behind the cute exterior." The typography is based on standard newspaper design and features Trade Gothic for titles and credits with Times Roman for body copy. The booklet is printed one-color on uncoated gray paper to replicate newsprint.

Product: CD
Client/Label: Cantaloupe Music
Artist: Gutbucket
Design: Another Limited Rebellion
Illustration: Sparkplugs
Photography: Alyssa Scheinson/istockphoto
Country: USA

Artwork

Digitaria

Eduardo Recife designed the cover for this debut album. "I got my inspiration from either the music or the lyrics. Since I had complete creative freedom, it was easier to make things flow naturally. The cover is about life, something along the lines of 'you reap what you sow,'" explains Recife. He used vector illustrations, contrasting this computer-generated imagery by printing it on a more "organic" type of stock. He created custom typefaces for the logo and cover text, and used FlashBoy on the reverse.

Product: CD
Client/Label: Gigolo Records
Artist: Digitaria
Design: Misprinted Type
Country: Brazil

Turkish Delight/Mighty Girl/
Boney M Down/Nummer Fire

"The images for the Lindstrøm and Prins Thomas compilations have been slow and sometimes painstaking to create, but the results are visually eye-catching with strong ideas behind them," explains designer Chris Bolton. "Without the concept, the graphics wouldn't be that strong." The Beatles' song *Norwegian Wood* inspired the idea for wooden images on the album artwork. "The decision to use animals on the covers was due to the fact that, like most Nordic countries, Norway has lots of woodland and forests," adds Bolton, "so I asked the guys to pick a few forest creatures and they chose the frog, squirrel, owl, salmon, and butterfly—not the typical moose or reindeer!" The wood illustrations came from a craftsman specializing in wood images. Bolton first provided him with vector line illustrations to work from; he crafted the images, and these were touched up in Photoshop.

Product: Vinyl
Client/Label: Eskimo Recordings/N.E.W.S.
Artist: Lindstrøm/Prins Thomas
Design: Chris Bolton
Illustration: Juha Nuuti/Chris Bolton
Country: Belgium

The End of the Beginning

Every year, the Copenhagen Consulting Company (CoCoCo) gives a CD compilation to its employees. re-public chooses the tracks, compiles the CD, and designs the cover. re-public produced *The End of the Beginning* following CoCoCo's logo redesign, which signaled the beginning of a new era for it. "Black was the color of its new identity. That is why I chose to use dark colors for the digipak and CD," explains Romeo Vidner. "It also looks serious and reflects its new corporate image, and I wanted to work with black surfaces, to see what effect I could create just using the same kind of color." The CD is made in black plastic and the artwork is silk-screen printed in black on top of it, which creates the look of real vinyl. The CD digipak features an ink image (that was shot in water) and the text, set in Gotham and Didot Regular, has been applied to it using a spot varnish.

Product: CD
Client: Copenhagen Consulting Company
Design: re-public
Country: Denmark

Katyou Fuugetsu

Emmi Salonen created an identity and this
CD packaging for the koto player and singer
Chieko Mori. "My solution was to use a pattern
from ancient Japanese drawings together with
modern Western typography and shapes,"
explains Salonen. "The identity suggests the
new approach to koto playing. Using only the
colors of the Japanese flag, red and white, it also
reflects the traditional origins of the instrument."
Emphasizing this, when you open the CD case,
it is pure white. The CD is set in red and all
photography is black and white—only Mori's
kimono remains red. Avant Garde Light has
been used for the text and logo font, together
with Shelley Volante Script as the subtitle font.
The contrasting cuts of the fonts also reflect
the mix of old and new in the music.

Product: CD
Client/Artist: Chieko Mori
Label: Felmay
Design: Emmi
Photography: Eva Assad
Countries: Italy/Japan/UK

Artwork

Post Rock Defends the Nation

Brad Kayal designed the CD package for this debut album. "The band's CD was nearing completion by the time I got the job of designing the packaging," explains Kayal. "Initial listens to various tracks had already started a buzz and the design needed to live up to already high expectations." Bon Savants wanted something other than the usual CD jewel case and that also pulled from Russian Constructivist artwork it had used in previous media. "Tying the titles of the album back to a Constructivist look seemed simple enough," explains Kayal. "I spent a bit of time looking through old posters and printing techniques before I finally decided I wanted to use both geometric art and halftone photographic images. In addition, since the packaging had multiple faces which could all be viewed independently, I approached a lot of it like a group of mini posters that also had to work as a group." Kayal produced all of the CD imagery, mostly inspired by the song lyrics.

Product: CD
Client/Artist: Bon Savants
Label: e to the i, pi
Design: Brad Kayal
Country: USA

Midnight Magic

Skatebård's music is influenced by Italo-disco and 1980s music. It is full of references: Ferrari, science fiction, tennis, modernism, futurism, VHS, love, laser, neon, UFO, boogie. Without trying to depict all of these visually striking references, the artwork has been made abstract, with a dripping mouth as its main element. This image, found in horror, disco, and heavy metal, with the already mentioned styles, symbols, and -isms, sums up who Skatebård is and what can be expected from him musically.

Product: CD
Client/Label: Digitalo Enterprises
Artist: Skatebård
Design: Grandpeople
Country: Norway

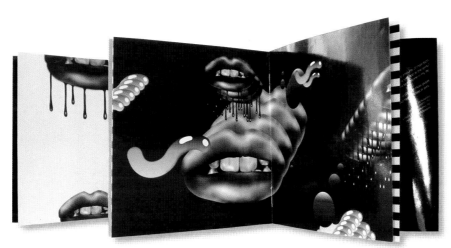

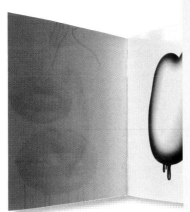

Glastonbury: The Movie

This is a three-DVD box set of Glastonbury music festival filmed in 1993—the last year of the great, "old-school" Glastonbury Festivals, before ATMs and cell phone towers came onsite. It is for everyone who never came to see what they missed, and for those who want to relive their festival experience. Airside created the package to represent the festival illustratively. As it did not want any type to interfere with the imagery, all credit information is on the package reverse. Its specially designed DVD logo has a retro influence.

Product: DVD
Client: Glastonbury
Design: Airside
Country: UK

War Frequencies

Jewboy designed the cover for this release that features various artists. "With all the Teder releases I get full creative freedom," he explains. "This is rather rare in the business, but worked perfectly for us, so there is no briefing, just 'listen to the music and do what you think best for it.'" The artists were asked to contribute to "the sound of war" as the album, titled *War Frequencies*, was about the Lebanese/Israeli war. The cover image was created with reference to the famous Doppler effect using a mix of digital and handmade imagery.

WAR FREQUENCIES   2006

Product: CD
Client/Label: Teder Music
Artist: Various
Design: Jewboy Corporation™
Country: Israel

The John Byrd E.P.

Jason Munn designed the packaging for this live EP. "The design is inspired by the fact that it is a live album and it is named after Death Cab for Cutie's soundman, John Byrd," explains Munn. "All the imagery I have used is based on the idea of recording. The tape reels are blue and pink to represent the idea that the song's content is often relationship related." Munn created the illustrations and complemented them with the use of Futura typeface. The packaging was printed using a simple four-color spot.

Product: CD
Client/Label: Barsuk Records
Client/Artist: Death Cab for Cutie
Design: The Small Stakes
Photography: Paul Schiek
Country: USA

Listen Up!

David Lane designed this cover. "Our brief was to produce a coherent set of branded packaging across all formats for the single and related promotional material," explains Lane. "The 7in picture disc used a crop of an existing image showing the singer Beth Ditto's bottom and legs in Lycra. The concept was to subvert mass-marketed glossy music imagery, and to question the ideals of beauty and body acceptance." The photograph also mirrored similar mainstream imagery that exploited the female body to sell predominantly male music. In contrast, the 7in vinyl had a glamorous crop of her face, printed in black and white, with the title and paint dripping from her hand and microphone overprinted in a fluorescent spot blue. This crudely branded the seemingly glossy image. Lane designed a custom title type for the single. The label copy and credits were set in Amasis.

Product: CD/Vinyl
Client/Label: Back Yard Recordings
Artist: Gossip
Design: David Lane
Country: UK

What's The Time Mr Wolf?

As deisgner David Lane explains, "The idea was to create two images, one showing a theatrical, overly directed sensationalist scene and the other to show the reality of it—duct tape, boxes, and cut paper. It came about because I wanted a way to show that the band were both well-taught music-school musicians and gritty, soulful rockers. Also, given that the project had a proper budget, we wanted to build a tight set." The title and band logo were cut from card and placed in the set as the only lettering in camera on the cover.

Product: CD
Client/Label: Mercury Music
Artist: The Noisettes
Art Direction: David Lane/Ollie Evans/Partizan
Design: Mercury Music
Photography: Daniel Alexander
Country: UK

Artwork

Bigboy Exercises

310k designed this record sleeve as a sort
of constructed mind spin of lines, plans, and
drawings. "The idea was to create an interesting
and semicomplicated technical line drawing
of connected machines and other elements,"
explains Ivo Schmetz. "In a way this could be
the technical drawing of the mind of Mason.
A complex collection of bits and pieces that
are somehow connected in an electric circuit."
VAG Rounded typeface has been used to
contrast with the lines of the illustration.

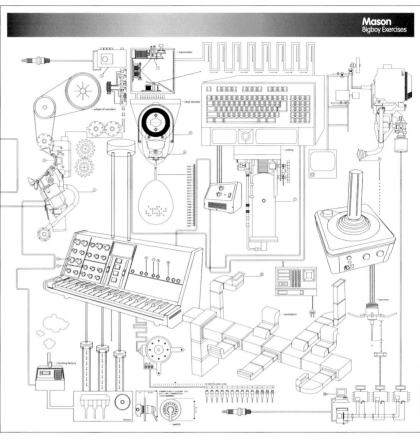

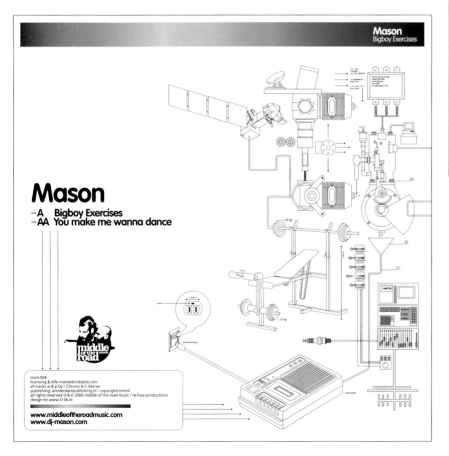

Product: Vinyl

Client/Artist: Mason

Label: Middle of the Road

Design: 310k

Country: The Netherlands

Where Were You?

Ricky Tillblad designed this cover. "The band did not want to be on the cover," explains Tillblad. "Instead they wanted something modern and clean, yet inspired by the 1960s." As classic pop groups also influenced the band, Tillblad wanted to create a straightforward cover that had an old vinyl album feel to it. "I was inspired by the soft shapes and feeling of the Velvet Underground cover *Loaded* and The Beatles cover *Yellow Submarine*." Tillblad created an illustration of an old vintage record player through which "colorful music flows." "It felt like a classic concept," he explains. "I kept the background white and clean to get a crisp feeling and to keep the focus on the illustration." BottleKaps typeface has been used with Avant Garde for the smaller credits.

Product: CD
Client/Artist: The Virtues
Label: Zip Records
Design: Zion Graphics
Country: Sweden

Hobby film showreel

This DVD package contains the showreel of the directors at Hobby Film. "They wanted a package that was not just a standard jewel case or slipcase, but something more memorable, yet not too expensive," explains Jonas Kjellberg. The package design follows Kjellberg's corporate identity design, which features a cute cartoon version of a horror theme complete with a skull for the letter "o." "The cover features the company logo that I created and then I have extended it to work with the packaging by creating this dripping blood imagery over the edges of the packaging," he explains. The package was used as a promotional piece and sent to various clients and advertising agencies.

Product: DVD
Client: Hobby Film
Design: Zion Graphics
Country: Sweden

Searching for a Former Clarity

"I was asked to create something dark with a timeless feel," explains Jason Munn. His cover imagery and design relate to the album's overall concept of darkness—whether in politics, the music industry, or life as a touring band. "I really wanted everything in the package to be black and white, the idea of 'clarity' being clearly black or white, with no in-betweens," adds Munn. The cover imagery uses Schiek's photographs, which were photocopied and then scanned. The whole package, which includes two vinyl discs, one black and one white, was printed in one color on uncoated stock.

Product: Vinyl
Client/Artist: Against Me!
Client/Label: Fat Wreck Chords
Design: The Small Stakes
Photography: Paul Schiek
Country: USA

Artwork

First Light's Freeze

"With the design of this package I was greatly inspired by the music and album title," explains Jason Munn. "Through the imagery used I have tried to show the idea of light, and of a cold, frosting over plants." The leaf imagery is clip art and the burst of light in the center of the cover was created by photocopying a photograph of the sun. The vinyl sits inside an inner sleeve, which also features a leaf image. Munn has used Akzidenz Grotesk throughout and the package has been printed on an uncoated stock.

Product: Vinyl
Client/Label: Asthmatic Kitty Records
Artist: Castanets
Design: The Small Stakes
Country: USA

In the Vines

Jason Munn's brief for this album cover was
fairly open, and he was greatly inspired by the
music he heard and the album title. "I wanted
to try to create something sparse, dark, and
beautiful for this album cover," he explains.
"I've used imagery of dead pressed plants
on the cover because I felt that although the
plants seem trampled on and battered, they
still remain beautiful. Castanets' music feels
similar to me—sparse, dark, and beautiful." Munn
used Scala typeface throughout the package,
which has been printed using two spot colors,
metallic gold and black, on uncoated stock. The
CD package "O" card features a blind emboss.

Product: CD/Vinyl
Client/Label: Asthmatic Kitty Records
Artist: Castanets
Design: The Small Stakes
Country: USA

My Book Laughs/
Weather Warning

Ewan Robertson created the artwork for this
CD single release. Having worked previously
with the band, Robertson wanted to continue
the same graphic design. "I decided to use the
front cover as a visual metaphor for the a-side
and the back cover for the b-side," explains
Robertson. "The front is a striking and comical
image whereas the back is similarly striking,
but serious. The same color palette was used to
unite the images, one photograph, one vector."

Product: CD
Client/Label: One Records
Artist: The Xcerts
Design: Ewan Robertson
Country: UK

Plans We Made

Stefan G. Bucher designed this CD cover.
As he explains, "John needed a visual calling
card. Instead of the standard singer/songwriter
headshot with sensitive-guy typography, I wanted
to do something illustrated and more intricate—
although we still wanted to have John on the
cover, as for indie artists this is still one of the
big ways of getting their face out there." Bucher
has created an illustrated image of McCarty
based on photos by Peter Batchelder and
Nathan Harrmann. The main cover type has
been assembled from an incomplete set of
clay display letters that Bucher bought at
a flea market, with all other type set in Helvetica.
"We printed the package on uncoated stock,
to get an instant vintage look," adds Bucher.

Product: CD
Client/Label: Burst Records
Artist: John McCarty
Design/Illustration: 344
Country: USA

Equilibrium

Christian Hundertmark designed the cover for
this album, released to celebrate Main Concept's
10th anniversary. "A lot of hip-hop covers are
pretty clichéd, showing the bands posing
together with graffiti-inspired typography,"
explains Hundertmark. "Since Main Concept
is a band with an intellectual background (the
frontman works as a doctor) and the content of
the songs is political, we thought that the cover
should also be something special and not follow
the standard hip-hop style of design." The idea
was to create typography using red duct tape
stuck to a wall and photograph the band in front
of it. Images showing elements of the tape were
then featured throughout the album. The cover
was printed four-color in a digipak format.

Product: CD
Client/Label: 58 Beats
Artist: Main Concept
Design: C100 Studio
Photography: Matthias Aletsee
Country: Germany

Penetrate the Empty Space

Hundertmark designed the package for the CD and vinyl versions of this album with the brief to create something fresh. "I had shot the photos of CCTV cameras, which I have used on the cover, when I was in London two years before and thought that they'd fit quite well with the band's name Intrudas and the album title *Penetrate the Empty Space*," explains Hundertmark. "It came from the idea that these cameras penetrate the empty space somehow too." Hundertmark created other graphic elements for the cover to complement the CCTV camera imagery. Isonorm Monospaced typeface was used and the package has been printed in four-color.

Product: CD/Vinyl
Client/Label: 58 Beats
Artist: Intrudas
Design: C100 Studio
Country: Germany

Minx

Hundertmark designed this album package. The cover artwork is a combination of Seidel's black-and-white photographs with other graphic elements created by C100 Studio. Some of the graphic elements, including the band name, have been applied to the package in orange and pink neon ink. The package is a six-panel digipak and Avant Garde typeface has been used throughout.

Product: CD
Client/Label: Compost Records/G-Stone Recordings
Artist: Marsmobil
Design: C100 Studio
Photography: Florian Seidel
Country: Germany

Artwork

091

Fire Stories

David Bailey designed the cover for this tour CD release. "Jon from Serfs chose brown variations of thick paper and asked me to make as many covers in a day as I could," he explains. "No text was needed on the front or back, and the band name was an optional inclusion." Bailey created largely improvised drawings after listening to the band's recording. He used mostly black ink with little color or small stencils from books to make black images, and Letraset rub-off letters to write "Serfs." "I wanted the drawings to be rough and for each cover to be different in terms of subject matter and coverage of ink," adds Bailey. "I was keen to smudge paints to create a printed-looking effect and have the ink look as if it has bled into each design. Layouts of each cover weren't planned in advance and it was left largely to chance what the cover would look like when folded to become a front and back housed in a plastic sleeve." Each of the limited run of 21 CDs has a one-off original pen-and-ink cover.

Product: CD
Client/Artist: Serfs
Design: David Bailey
Country: UK

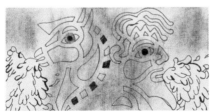

Artwork

093

Heat Exchange

Paul Roberts and Dom Cooper designed this CD and vinyl single cover. The band's shows feature heavy use of projected visuals in the form of short films, random cine footage, and animations, and the design brief was to incorporate these images within the sleeve. "The main idea is to reference the cinematic side of the band's personality," explains Roberts. "Using nostalgic 1970s images complements the band's modern approach and vocals, and fits the mood and feel of the music." The images came from old cine footage belonging to the band and their families. Antique Bold typeface has been used on the cover, the colors for which were picked from the colors within the deckchair and grass.

Product: CD/Vinyl
Client/Label: Sugarlow Records
Artist: The Electric Cinema
Design: Paul Roberts/Dom Cooper
Country: UK

Improv and Collaboration

"The band suggested a colorful floral-based design with little or no white space," explains David Bailey. "They were also keen to have as little writing on the record cover as possible; only the band name, and the record label logo on the back, were needed. In addition the band play with homemade instruments and the music is largely improvised so I decided to draw flowers from memory rather than work from photographs or life." Bailey worked in patterns and elements of repetition that he felt reflected the drone and looping sounds of Neptune's music. He drew all the artwork straight onto paper with pen; inked, penciled, painted, or crayoned colors on top; then reinked certain parts to add emphasis and balance the weight of the front sleeve. "I wanted the colors to be bright and psychedelic to suit the music and the heaviness and lack of space of the drawings."

Product: Vinyl
Client/Artist: Neptune
Label: Golden Lab Records
Design: David Bailey
Country: UK

Content

Waiting For A God

Paul Roberts' vinyl packaging design for this release echoed the look and feel of the video created for the single. It used the yellow and black color system that is on all The New Shapes' artwork and branding. "I had directed, designed, and animated the video for *Waiting For A God* so the idea for the sleeve artwork was to tie everything in together," explains Roberts. "So solid yellow was used as well as rotoscoped stills of each band member that were taken from the video and used on the sleeves." The imagery has been complemented with simple, clean typography to let the band members' images stand out.

Product: Vinyl
Client/Label: Pop Records
Artist: The New Shapes
Design: Paul Roberts
Country: UK

/05

"The client asked me to use the visual that you see here," explains Hideki Nakajima. "The image is of a crashed file of a photograph that Ryuichi Sakamoto took some years ago." Nakajima has used the image to cover the package almost entirely, leaving just the top part blank to apply the artist's name in a specially drawn typeface. The cover has been printed using six colors: four regular and two luminescent.

Product: CD
Client/Label: Warner Music Japan
Artist: Ryuichi Sakamoto
Design: Hideki Nakajima
Country: Japan

Blues & Reds

Purple Haze Studio designed this 12in vinyl
sleeve. "The main idea behind the design was
to create an arty illustration, or collage, that
emphasized the different musical styles on
the album in a visual way," explains Clemens
Baldermann. "The design was inspired by
modern paintings by artists like Cy Twombly
and Robert Ryman. It was created by using
a number of different hand-drawn elements
and included the use of ink, watercolor paints,
pencil and brush, and silk screen." The covers
were printed in full color and also feature spot
color. Cooper typeface was used for the credit
texts on the sleeve.

Product: Vinyl
Client/Label: Cityslang
Artist: Justine Electra
Design: Purple Haze Studio
Country: Germany

Forbidden Fruit Part 2

"The idea for this design was to create bold,
individual typography in conjunction with
illustrations to create a unique and strong
visibility that underlines the limited-edition
character of the vinyl records series," explains
Baldermann. "A custom-made title type, old-
fashioned floral illustrations, and vector and
3D illustrations have been used to create the
artwork—a gross mixture of illustration styles
like the gross mixture of sample and instrumental
styles on the records series." All of the artwork
elements were designed in-house apart from
the copyright-free old-fashioned illustrations
and clip art. Clarendon typeface was used for
credit texts inspired by old-fashioned labels,
nameplates, and religious icon pictures.

Product: Vinyl
Client/Label: Sellwell Records
Artist: Peabird & Tomahawk
Design: Purple Haze Studio
Country: Germany

Playtime is Over

Oscar Bauer, Ewan Robertson, and Eat Sleep Work/Play created the packages for these CD and vinyl releases. Their design is a straightforward visual metaphor for the title. "We have removed the play by removing the primary colors associated with it, which makes quite a striking and slightly humorous image," explains Bauer. "To avoid including text within the images, we have used stickers on top of the jewel case with the title; to continue the blackout theme, we used a gloss black inner tray; and for the first edition, black on both sides of the CD." Removing the gloss black inner tray reveals a small hidden picture. Choussat designed the "chalk writing" that has been used for the title and track listings.

Product: CD/Vinyl
Client/Label: Big Dada Recordings
Artist: Wiley
Design: Eat Sleep Work/Play with Oscar Bauer and Ewan Robertson
Photography: Per Crepin
Typography: Antoine Choussat
Country: UK

Rabbit

This limited-edition DVD features the animated
short *Rabbit* with a brief documentary on its
making, plus deleted scenes. *Rabbit* was created
using a collection of 1950s educational stickers
as source material, and the package design
kept that theme. The case directly refers to the
original envelopes that packaged the stickers,
found in a junk store in the early 1980s, and
also the covers of Ladybird books. The original
artwork was illustrated by Geoffrey Higham.
The fonts used are a combination of the original
typeface featured on the stickers, and Gill Sans,
which is very similar. Each DVD is hand-stamped
and numbered on the reverse in two inks.

Product: DVD
Client: Sclah Films
Artist: Run Wrake
Design: Run Wrake
Country: UK

Saisons 3 & 4

pleaseletmedesign "physically" created two albums that formed a single object for this release. "The back of one part serves as the front of the other, together forming a mimetically reversible album," explains Damien Aresta. "Funk Sinatra are a little bit crazy so we decided to show their universe within the album cover. The idea was based on taking photographs to create this universe." Akkurat and Enabler typefaces have been used throughout.

Product: CD
Client/Label: Home Records
Artist: Funk Sinatra
Design: pleaseletmedesign
Photography: Victor Laval/pleaseletmedesign
Country: Belgium

Songs The Bonzo Dog Band Taught Us: A Pre-history of The Bonzos

Product: CD
Client/Label: Lightning Tree
Artist: Various
Design: Dan Abbott
Country: UK

Dan Abbott created this compilation package of novelty jazz songs from the 1920s and 1930s. "The idea for the package came from the music, which is the way I like to work," he explains. "I wanted the final illustration to reflect the typically conservative, yet at times deeply odd and surreal mood of many of the songs, hence the large pipe-smoking fish that the gentleman is carrying under his arm." To complement the cover illustration, Abbott has created a hand-drawn typeface for the text.

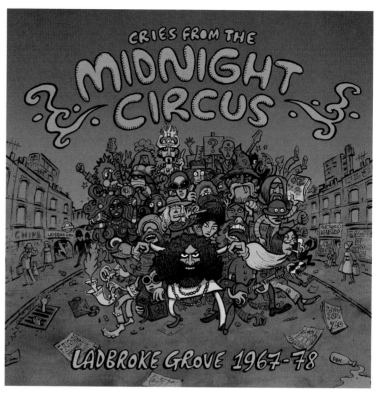

Cries From The Midnight Circus: Ladbroke Grove 1967–78

Product: CD
Client/Label: Sanctuary Records/
Castle Music
Artist: Various
Design: Dan Abbott
Country: UK

Dan Abbott's brief for this package was to produce illustrations and designs inspired by the music. "The music was a collection of recordings from bands loosely connected to West London's Ladbroke Grove 'scene,' which was a hotbed of cultural and musical revolution in the early 1970s," he explains. "I wanted to depict the Day-Glo and crazed nature of the counterculture in contrast with day-to-day London." Abbott created ink and pencil illustrations, which were later colored in Photoshop. He has used a hand-drawn typeface throughout.

Merit—Queen Of Swedish Hammond Folk Groove

Abbott and Sweden Graphics designed this retrospective compilation album package with the brief to create a cover that had a 1970s Swedish feel—referencing the time when Hemmingson made her most pivotal music—combined with a more contemporary aesthetic confirming that her music is still relevant today. Abbott found inspiration for the cover illustrations in the iconic fantasy images of Swedish artist Hans Arnold, also popular in the 1970s, and Swedish folk art. He created his own style of illustration using ink and pencil line drawings that were later colored in Illustrator. New Century Schoolbook typeface was used for all cover text.

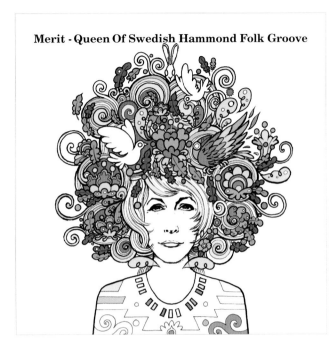

Product: CD
Client/Label: Bonnier Amigo
Artist: Merit Hemmingson
Design: Dan Abbott with Sweden Graphics
Country: Sweden

Birdman Ray

NB: Studio created this debut CD album
packaging with the brief to keep it simple and
cost-effective. The design features woodcut
illustrations of a bird, a human skeleton, and
a manta ray, which are a visual interpretation
of the album title and artist's name. The three
images have been lined up so that they became
one single figure, creating a strong cover image.
The typography was kept simple and clear as
the image effectively also visually spelt out the
name as a rebus. The package also features
a concertina folded inlay.

Product: CD
Client/Artist: Birdman Ray
Design: NB: Studio
Country: UK

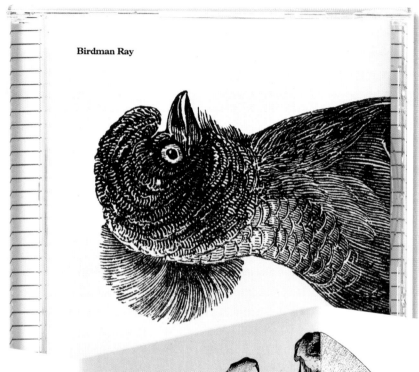

Birdman Ray

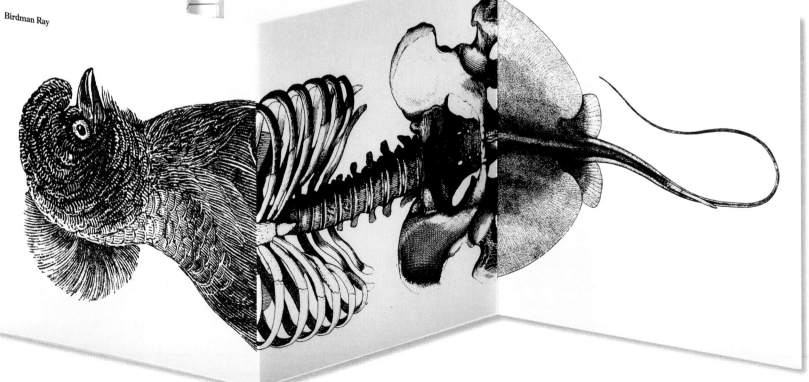

Birdman Ray

Hush Boy

No Days Off designed this cover. "We wanted to continue the 'space collage' theme of *Crazy Itch Radio* (shown below), and did so with a combination of graphic objects and still-life photography," explains Patrick Duffy. "We had some fun with these elements on the reverse of the sleeves, with stars spilling from lips and shooting out from fingers." Bold and classic Lubalin were used to offset the oddness of the imagery.

Crazy Itch Radio

"This brief was very open," explains Patrick Duffy. "All we were given was the title. Everything was based on our interpretation of those three words. The idea of the dog radio just came from thinking about what a crazy itch radio would look like. Dogs have a great scratching technique, and the idea of a dog with the body of a radio just seemed to fit perfectly. We hadn't heard the album until very late in the design process, but we knew it was going to be more 'pop' than its predecessor (*Kish Kash*), so we tried to make the DogRadio fun and friendly rather than weird and scary." Some simple, but colorful typography set in Lubalin has been used to complete the sleeve. For the limited-edition double LP (shown here), foil blocking was used to apply the band's logo.

Product: Vinyl
Client/Label: XL Recordings
Artist: Basement Jaxx
Design: No Days Off
Hand model: Carla Holdforth
Country: UK

Product: CD/Vinyl
Client/Label: XL Recordings
Artist: Basement Jaxx
Design: No Days Off
Photography: John Short
Country: UK

Artwork

LINE Series 3

These are Richard Chartier's sleeve designs for a variety of artists included in LINE's third series of work by international sound artists and composers, exploring the aesthetics of contemporary and digital minimalism. Since 2000 Chartier has documented compositional and installation work. "Artists commissioned to do works for LINE know the template for the packaging in advance," explains Chartier. "I work with the artists to find a suitable or evocative image to relate singly to the sonic work contained within the CD." This third series design was inspired by document folders, and each CD has a color-coded tag, or tab, on the front and back. Humanist typeface has been used throughout these releases, which are limited to a run of between 500 and 1,000.

Product: CD
Client/Label: LINE
Artist: Various
Art Direction/Design: Richard Chartier
Country: USA

Shockout Vol. 2:
Oppositional Ambitions

Slang designed this CD packaging with an open brief. It created the artwork by first printing out all the packaging content, then enlarging it on a photocopier, pasting it on street walls, and photographing it. The idea was to express the album title, *Oppositional Ambitions*, by using the illegally pasted street poster method. In addition, all material has been photocopied in black and white in order to contrast with its surroundings. The imagery is the label's two symbols, the lion head logo and electric shock symbol. Machine typeface has been used throughout.

Product: CD
Client/Label: Shockout
Artist: Various
Design: Slang
Country: USA

Mafia

Jan Oksbøl Callesen designed this album cover after discussions with the band about the album songs and what they meant, and Crunchy Frog's brief that the cover artwork contain images of the band. Callesen created a series of images that represents the content of the tracks. This sits together with track listings and credits created using hand-drawn type.

Product: CD/Vinyl

Client/Label: Crunchy Frog

Artist: epo-555

Design: Gul Stue

Country: Denmark

Red Light Don't Stop/Get Up/ Dirty Basement/Classic Cliché

No Days Off designed the packaging for this album, subsequent 12in singles, and promos with the brief summed up in two words: modern psychedelia. "We took the idea of modern psychedelia and filtered it through children's TV shows and Eduardo Paolozzi to create an aesthetic that suited the Elektrons' music," explains Duffy. "Each single sleeve can be seen as a journey: *Dirty Basement* takes us out from the club up onto the street; *Get Up* moves into a more pastoral scene to match the positive vibe of the track; and *Classic Cliché* takes us out into space and into an imagined utopia." The album featured an upside-down traffic light, and the designers used a red, amber, and green color scheme to denote each single release, keeping everything within the same color system. In addition, within the gatefold of the LP, two "information spirals" were created, one to contain all the songwriting credits, the other to detail each element used within the collage. All the sleeves were printed on uncoated board, the feel of which matched the look of the graphics.

Product: CD/Vinyl
Client/Label: Wall Of Sound
Artist: Elektrons
Design: No Days Off
Country: UK

Umun

Studio Poana created this album packaging. "We had no concept as such in mind when we began designing the cover," explain Thibault Choquel and Nicolas Dhennin. "We knew though that we wanted the cover to be abstract and unique." The result is a cover that features several different, yet connected abstract illustrations on both the inner and outer sleeves as well as the CD itself. In addition, Studio Poana created a new typeface for the band's logotype.

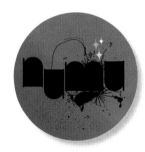

Product: CD
Client/Label: Waz Recordz
Artist: Numu
Design: Studio Poana
Country: France

The Big Chill

Vault49's brief was to represent the happy
energy and ambience of The Big Chill music
festival with recognizable visual references.
The cover imagery features an illustration that
incorporates items such as The Big Chill music
stages, speakers, wildlife, and trees, all of which
are synonymous with The Big Chill festival.
Inside, a foldout booklet contains actual scenes
from the event, which many who were there,
or have been, would recognize. The package
used recycled paper.

13. Roisin Murphy 'Through Time'
14. Emiliana Torrini 'Today Has Been OK'
15. Max Richter 'Written On The Sky'
16. Infantjoy 'Ghosts'
17. Tim Hardin 'Reason To Believe'
18. John Martyn 'Bless The Weather'
19. Jamie Lidell 'Multiply (In A Minor Key – Gonzales Remix)'
20. Nightmares On Wax 'I Am You'
21. Nitin Sawhney 'Sunset'
22. Boards of Canada 'Oscar See Through Red Eye'

Disc 2
1. Tonto's Expanding Head Band 'Cybernaut'
2. The Ukulele Orchestra of Great Britain 'Le Freak'
3. Quantic Soul Orchestra 'Get A Move On'
4. Husky Rescue 'Summertime Cowboy'
5. Ulrich Schnauss 'In All The Wrong Places'
6. Sparks 'Perfume'
7. Neon Heights 'Listen To The Music'
8. Bent 'Sing Me'
9. The Rebirth 'This Journey In'
10. Nuyorican Soul 'I Am The Black Gold Of The Sun' (4 Hero Remix)
11. Deniece Williams 'Free'
12. Eva Abraham 'Today and Everyday'
13. Nancy Wallace 'Are You Ready For Love?
14. The Lovin' Spoonful 'Daydream'
15. Harpers Bizarre '59th Street Bridge Song (Feelin' Groovy)'
16. Rodrigo y Gabriela 'Stairway To Heaven'
17. El Perro Del Mar 'God Knows (You Gotta Give to Get)'
18. Nick Drake 'Hazey Jane I'

Selection and sequencing by Pete Lawrence

Mastering by: Craig Dormer for Red Light Mastering Ltd. www.red-light.co.uk
RESISTCD78 p 2006 Resist Music Ltd © 2006 Resist Music Ltd
Distribution: SRD Tel: +44 (0)20 8802 3000 Made In England MCPS LC13816
Website: www.resist-music.co.uk Email: mailbox@resist-music.co.uk

THE BiGCHiLL RESIST.
www.bigchill.net

8 42694 02078 6

Product: CD
Client/Label: Resist
Artist: Various
Design: Vault49
Countries: UK/USA

Artwork

113

Made of Bricks

Richard Robinson worked with several other
creatives to produce this CD package. A series of
small sets were designed and then photographed,
including that of a house, the rooms of which
represented Kate Nash's musical inspiration,
which is mainly personal and homegrown.
Elements and illustrations within the rooms
relate to the song lyrics. Macdonald designed
and built the sets, and Clare Nash photographed
the objects and personal items relating to the
lyrics. These, along with Dockrill's black-and-
white illustrations of the lyrics, were cut out
and incorporated into the sets. Short then photographed Kate Nash in various poses, which he
directed with Macdonald. These were cut out
and placed within the models, and then shot
by Short in their entirety. All type used on the
package was handwritten by Dockrill.

Product: CD
Client/Label: Fiction/Polydor Ltd. (UK)
Artist: Kate Nash
Art Direction/Set Design: Chrissie Macdonald
Design: Richard Robinson
Illustration: Laura Dockrill
Photography: John Short/Clare Nash
Country: UK

Earth To America

Chris Bilheimer designed this CD package. "Since the idea of the album *Earth to America* was about trying to connect with a country that seemed to have been thrown off course by war, about peace and communication, the idea of a peace dove as a carrier pigeon made perfect sense," he explains. He created the dove images on the package. A booklet continues the dove theme, and features illustrated portraits of the band. One of the main requirements of the design was that it contained as little plastic as possible, so a board digipak package was used. Bilheimer chose Antique Extended for the typeface as he wanted something that was reminiscent of a typewriter to keep with the theme of old-fashioned communication methods.

Product: CD
Client/Label: Sanctuary
Artist: Widespread Panic
Design: Chris Bilheimer
Country: USA

Long Time Coming

Sopp Collective's brief for this cover was for it to reflect the acoustic-based pop music. "The album features beautiful melodies and harmonies; it is very organic, honest, and dynamic, yet timeless," explains Katja Hartung. "Since the band name suits their music very well, I headed toward playing with leaves as a starting point." The bands' portrait was made using actual leaves, collected and sorted by color to become part of a 2 × 3m (6½ × 9⅞ft) floor piece which took three days to assemble. This was photographed and applied to the digipak CD cover. Typography was kept to a minimum on the cover—just a simple logotype of the band's name and the album title—so as not to overpower the imagery.

Product: CD

Client/Artist: The Falls (Simon Rudston-Brown/ Melinda Kirwin)

Design: Sopp Collective

Photography: Richard Dobson

Country: Australia

Strictly Rhythm series

Peter Chadwick designed the packaging for this series of releases for the relaunched Strictly Rhythm label. His brief was to create packaging that had a gritty, urban feel. The imagery created for and used throughout the Strictly Rhythm sleeves is of various decaying street scenes mixed with a series of commissioned paintings by Barras. "The idea was to create images that hark back to the classic New York urban image of the early 1990s when Strictly Rhythm first started," explains Chadwick. "The use of more painterly and colorful illustration elevates the imagery above the normal graffiti look and brings it up-to-date." Although the packaging is fairly standard, uncoated stocks and white reverse board stock have been used to allow the inks to spread a little and thus give a less polished feel to the package. Sans Thirteen Black and Clarendon typefaces were used.

Product: CD/Vinyl
Client/Label: Strictly Rhythm
Artist: Various
Design: Popular
Illustration: Will Barras
Photography: Franck Sauvaire
Country: UK

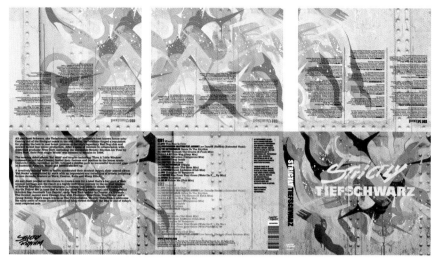

TODD TERRY
ALL STARS
Get Down

Featuring
Kenny Dope
DJ Sneak
Terry Hunter
& Tara Mcdonald

LOVE & HAPPINESS (Yemaya Y Ochùn)
A1.MAW ORIGINAL REMIX Short
A2.KENLOU DUB
B1.MASTERS AT WORK DUB
B2.MAW ORIGINAL REMIX DJ TOOL
WWW.STRICTIX.COM

RIVER OCEAN FEAT. INDIA
Love & Happiness
(Yemaya Y Ochùn)
MAW 2007 REMIXES

CONAN LIQUID
BRING IT BACK VOL.1

CONAN LIQUID
A1.BRING IT BACK
A2.BRING IT BACK (DJ Tool)
B1.YEYO'S GROOVE
B2.KEYS OF TIME
WWW.STRICTIX.COM

In the Mind of Jamie Cullum

This CD features Cullum's compilation of tracks that have influenced his music, including some personal favorites and two previously unreleased tracks by Cullum himself. Chadwick designed the packaging with the brief to avoid using a standard jewel case and to create a package that had a textural feel to it. He chose to use a CD digipak format as this made the release more book-like, enabling the viewer to open out the package to reveal the text and imagery. Willoughby's cover illustration shows Cullum looking upward while floating around his head are images of items that he likes and that have inspired him, creating a visual reference that is directly linked into the album title.

Product: CD
Client/Label: District 6
Artist: Jamie Cullum/Various
Design: Popular
Illustration: Paul Willoughby
Country: UK

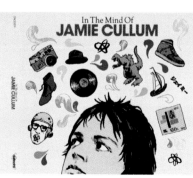

Jape is Grape

Lidström and Bolger designed this packaging for Jape. "We have been working with Jape for the past couple of years, producing all his printed material, photography, and most recently we codirected his music video for *Floating*," explains Lidström. "When we design for Jape we always try to create an air of dark humor so that although the visual style may change, the core feeling remains. We try to portray him as this unlucky character who gets into odd and surreal situations through no fault of his own." The idea for the design shown here is based on the use of photo boards, similar to those found at the seaside. The difference here though is that the theme of the board is a little darker and more surreal, fitting Jape's existing aesthetic. "The cover image depicts Jape falling, or floating, to his death through the sky just after being dropped from the claws of a giant blackbird," adds Lidström. "This motion references the title of the lead track, *Floating*." Hand-rendered type and Century Gothic have been used throughout.

Product: CD/Vinyl
Client/Label: V2 Records
Artist: Jape
Design: M&E
Country: Ireland

RMNMN

This EP contains five tracks, each individually written, performed, and produced by the five band members. "I wanted to emphasize the individual approach taken in the writing and production of this record, focusing on each member's piece separately," explains Bolger. "I began by illustrating icons that represent different types of sound, then broke them down into categories: acoustic, voice, drone, sample, effect, electric, beat, bass, and percussion. I then gave each band member a sheet of these icons and asked them to choose the ones they felt represented their music the best. From this I pieced together an illustration for each song. These five illustrations were used as song titles on the back cover and combined to make up the illustration on the front."

Product: CD
Client/Label: Greyslate Records
Artist: The Redneck Manifesto
Design: M&E
Country: Ireland

Earth To Atlanta

Bilheimer designed this package for the movie of Widespread Panic's show at the Fox Theater in Atlanta, USA. "The Fox Theater is a unique venue that is very important to the band and so they wanted it featured on the cover of the package," he explains. For the cover image, Bilheimer created an illustration of the venue, distressed it, and added a stained paper texture to it. Downcome typeface has been used to apply the title to the package.

Product: CD/DVD
Client/Label: Sanctuary Records
Artist: Widespread Panic
Design: Chris Bilheimer
Country: USA

Moog Acid

As Jon Forss of Non-Format explains, "We were given an open brief to produce appropriate packaging. We had seen the miniature synth models of Dan McPharlin via a design blog and knew his work would be perfect as imagery for *Moog Acid*." Non-Format commissioned McPharlin to produce a series of new Moog models, which he then photographed for use on the album. A typeface was created for the cover inspired by late 1960s typefaces such as Countdown and Data 70. The teardrop shape is inspired by the word "Acid" in the title. "We were keen for Dan's images to take center stage so we positioned all of the type onto the back of the packaging and kept the front clear of any type," adds Forss. The CD version sits inside a slipcase and the LP has a gatefold sleeve.

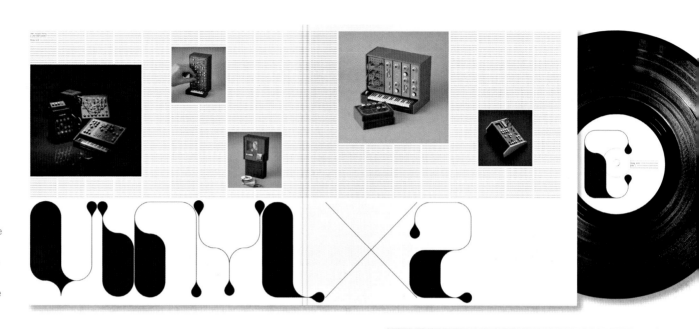

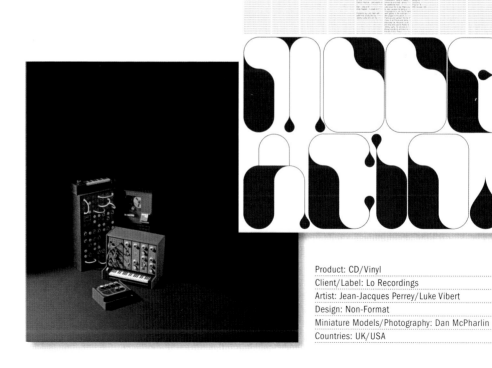

Product: CD/Vinyl
Client/Label: Lo Recordings
Artist: Jean-Jacques Perrey/Luke Vibert
Design: Non-Format
Miniature Models/Photography: Dan McPharlin
Countries: UK/USA

Artwork

Nouvelle Vague

The release of Nouvelle Vague's debut album was one of Peacefrog's first forays into non-dance material so Dylan Kendle's package design had to feel part of the stable, but have its own character. *Nouvelle Vague* translates both as "New Wave" and "Bossa Nova," and the album songs feature various female vocalists; however, they were talented session musicians rather than band members (in the traditional sense), so while there was now perceivably a "face," it wasn't just one singer. "To reflect this, and the music, I wanted the artwork to be a marriage of two conflicting styles, so geometric handcut monospace type sat against wistful 'idealized' illustrations of the girls," explains Kendle. Deacon supplied the cover illustrations, and handcut paper type was used with Helvetica Compressed. The package was printed CMYK with a spot metallic and gloss laminate finish, and a limited-edition white vinyl 12in single was also produced.

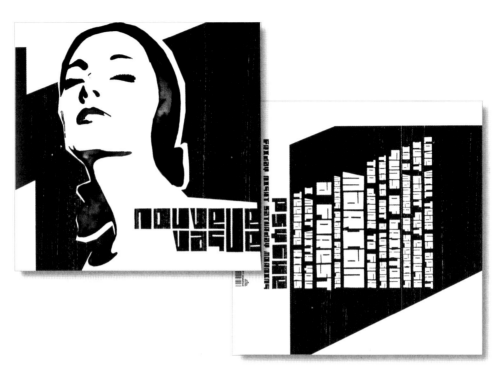

Product: Vinyl
Client/Label: Peacefrog
Artist: Nouvelle Vague
Design: Dylan Kendle
Illustration: Giles Deacon
Country: UK

Fantastic Playroom

"The band take on lots of different references musically and I had the challenge of conveying this into the sleeve," Richard Robinson explains. "Both myself and the photographer had put forward some visuals for the band to consider, and we both referenced the styling of Roxy Music… the band were into this idea, but also wanted to explore some other directions." On the day of the shoot, Robinson and Chalkley tried out several different styles for the band and the image seen here was chosen. "We hadn't really expected to use these shots for the sleeve," adds Robinson, "but once we got the contact sheets back, it was clear that this was a really iconic set." The image was then treated to give it a less sleek finish. The title is set in a custom font based on old breakdancing sleeves. This works alongside Gil Sans Light for body copy.

Product: Vinyl
Client/Label: Island/Modular
Artist: New Young Pony Club
Design: Richard Robinson
Photography: Dean Chalkley
Country: UK

Product: CD
Client/Label: Music For Dreams
Artist: Hess Is More (aka Mikkel Hess)
Design: Cyklon
Country: Denmark

Captain Europe/Yes Boss mixes

The Music for Dreams label has a standardized format for the cover layout with a black-and-white bar (containing label name, catalog number, and bar code), which is also printed across the actual CD. With this, Cyklon created all other artwork for the cover, based on the title *Captain Europe*, depicting a reimagined Europe using a style that reflected the electronically generated music. "Technical illustrations, such as rail maps and circuits, inspired the form of the drawing," explains Henrik Gytz. "Rail maps are an abstract way of portraying an area and its connectedness and the idea of using circuits came from opening up the old 1970s keyboards Hess is More used on the album." The illustrations were drawn in Illustrator using a quadratic grid and Range and OCR-F typefaces have been used for their distinctive technical appearance and geometric shapes. The illustrative and typographic idea has been carried through to the *Yes Boss* single remixes CD.

Eurolove

Stephane Manel and Jean-Marie Delbes created this artwork with the brief to create a package that was both "sexy and curious." "We were inspired by some hedonistic images that we found from the 1920s and 1930s," explains Manel. "The resultant package is a kind of mix of 1930s images and drawings in a 1970s style." The cover mixes new illustrations with found imagery, and a font Delbes created specifically for use on the cover.

Product: CD
Client/Label: Record Makers
Artist: Hypnolove
Design: Stephane Manel/Jean-Marie Delbes
Country: France

Silent Sound

Chris Bigg and Vaughan Oliver at v23 designed this special package, which was limited to just 1,000 numbered and signed copies. It features a live recording by J. Spaceman at St. George's Hall in Liverpool, UK, and was produced just five minutes after the end of the performance. v23 was commissioned to visualize the notion of Silent Sound within the packaging design. The result is a tactile package printed on uncoated board, and much of the imagery has been taken from architectural details found within the hall where the CD was recorded. The 350 people attending the performance were each presented with a copy of the CD to slot into the back of their printed program as they left the hall.

Product: CD
Client/Label: A Foundation
Artist: Iain Forsyth & Jane Pollard/J. Spaceman
Design: v23
Country: UK

Blinded by the Sun

Dan Abbott's brief for this album packaging was to design something as intense as the music. "On a simple level the album's title, *Blinded by the Sun*, brings to mind both eyes and the sun so I decided that it would be fun to utilize a lot of circular shapes on the packaging, suggesting both items," explains Abbott. "We opted for a whiteout look so on the front cover the band's name only appears on a sticker. The color white reflects the idea of brightness and of blindness." Abbott created the imagery for the cover by designing and building a large sculpture, which he then photographed. A hand-drawn typeface has been used throughout the package.

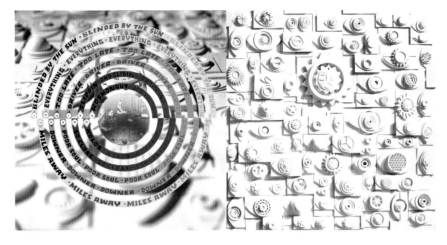

Product: CD
Client/Label: Molten
Artist: On Trial
Design: Dan Abbott
Country: UK

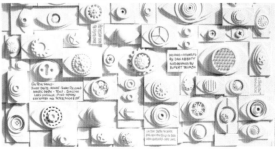

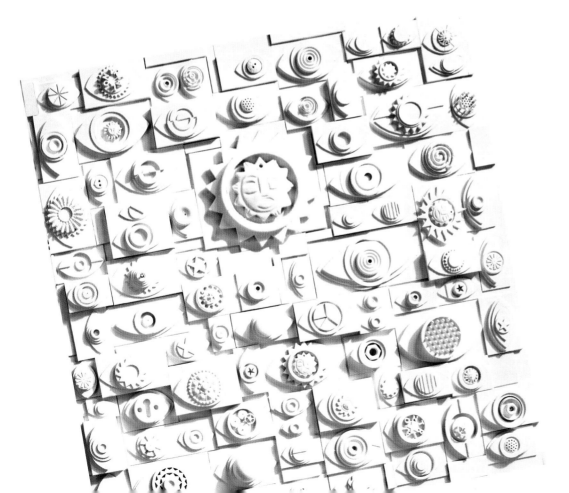

Industry/Jane Falls Down

"The band are an interesting mixture of 1980s electro pop with burlesque cabaret, so within the design of the packaging, and of the overall campaign, we wanted to create a sense of theatrics," explains designer Paul West. "We did this by way of exaggerated posturing from the band combined with 'industry' images such as modernist collages and Bauhaus architecture, airplanes, and machinery." Form created The Modern rubber stamps and a postage stamp to use on the packaging. These will change with every release, but remain central to the campaign as a whole.

Product: CD
Client/Label: Mercury Records (Universal)
Artist: The Modern
Design: Form
Photography: Darron Coppin
Country: UK

John Peel: Right Time, Wrong Speed (1977–1987)

This CD features a collection of indie tracks as championed by the late John Peel on his radio show between 1977 and 1987. "I decided that a portrait by Sir Peter Blake would be a fitting tribute," explains Scott Parker. "We wanted to create a respectful cover to John's memory." Blake's watercolor portrait sits on the cover with minimal type set in Avant Garde and neatly contained in a box in the top-left corner, giving Blake's portrait its rightful space. The painting was produced in a limited run of 50 prints to use as promotional items.

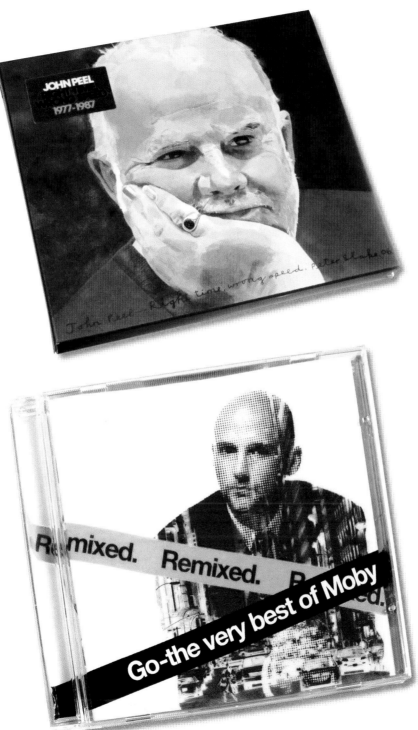

Product: CD
Client/Label: WMTV
Artist: Various
Design: Scott Parker Design
Portrait: Peter Blake
Country: UK

Go—The Very Best of Moby Remixed

This release features some of Moby's best-selling tracks, remixed by some of the world's best-known and most respected producers. GraphicTherapy designed the packaging with the brief to get away from the original release. "The images were changed dramatically by combining illustration and photography," explains David Calderley. "The artist wanted the imagery to be bright and uncompromising to reflect the energy of the record." The photographs used for the album were originally taken in New York by Clinch. Helvetica Bold typeface was used.

Product: CD
Client/Label: Mute
Artist: Moby
Design: GraphicTherapy
Photography: Danny Clinch
Country: USA

For Mother/Room 337

Richard Robinson designed these 12in vinyl covers. "The music is atmospheric, minimal techno and, when I heard it, I instantly thought of Jim Green's photographic series taken in Iceland," explains Robinson. "The barren landscapes with unusual 'sculptures' seem to carry the same message as the music—beautiful, but still slightly off-balance." The photography was not commissioned specifically and was Green's personal project that Robinson asked to use. The sleeves have been printed matte with a spot UV finish on the front panel, and a reworked version of Einstein typeface has been used throughout.

Product: Vinyl
Client/Label: Peacefrog
Artist: Aril Brikha
Design: Richard Robinson
Photography: Jim Green
Country: UK

Guitarrazón

Alfalfa created an original pen-and-ink illustration, inspired by the idea of "the way of the guitar," for the album packaging. "The illustration started with elements of a guitar, but just as the 'guitar determines where the music will take you,' I wanted to let the guitar determine where the illustration would take me," explains Rafael Esquer. "The illustration was created freely while listening to the music and I think the result is a fresh, vibrant composition." To complement the illustration, the classic and organic Eva typeface has been used. In addition to the album design, Alfalfa also created a series of promotional posters and postcards.

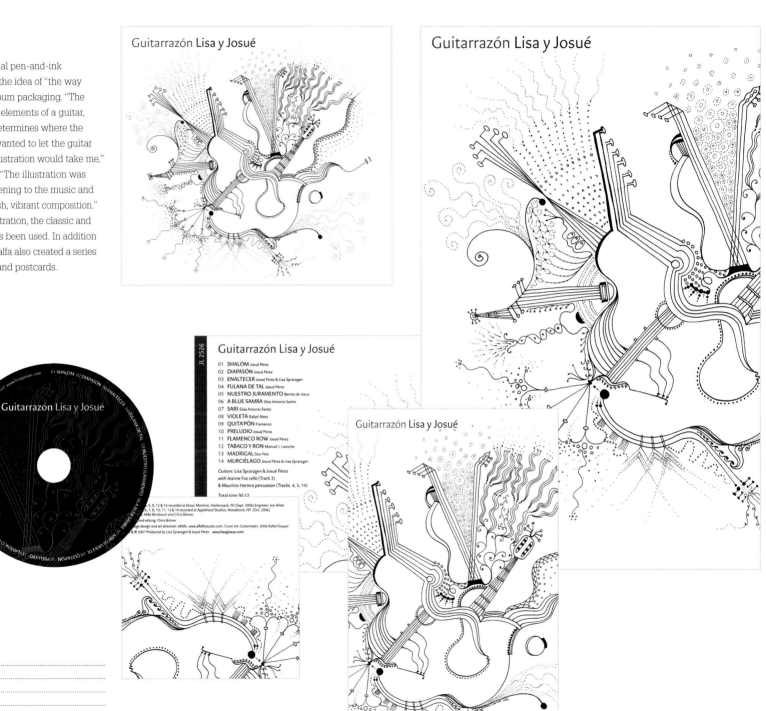

Guitarrazón Lisa y Josué

JL 2526

01 SHALOM Josué Pérez
02 DIAPASÓN Josué Pérez
03 ENALTECER Josué Pérez & Lisa Spraragen
04 FULANA DE TAL Josué Pérez
05 NUESTRO JURAMENTO Benito de Jesus
06 A BLUE SAMBA Silas Antonio Santo
07 SARI Silas Antonio Santo
08 VIOLETA Rafael Alers
09 QUITA'PÓN Flamenco
10 PRELUDIO Josué Pérez
11 FLAMENCO ROW Josué Pérez
12 TABACO Y RON Manuel J. Laroche
13 MADRIGAL Don Felo
14 MURCIÉLAGO Josué Pérez & Lisa Spraragen

Guitars: Lisa Spraragen & Josué Pérez
with Jeanne Fox cello (Track 3)
& Mauricio Herrera percussion (Tracks 4, 5, 14)

Total time 50:12

Product: CD/DVD
Client/Artist: Lisa y Josué
Design: Alfalfa Studio
Illustration: Rafael Esquer
Country: USA

Artwork

129

A Bugged Out Mix by Klaxons

Richard Robinson designed the packaging for this double CD compiled and mixed by Jamie Reynolds of the Klaxons. "One of Reynolds' interests is art; he had an integral role in the design of their own album and wanted to have input into this project. He had this image already and thought it would be perfect to use on the sleeve," explains Robinson. "So then what I had to do was work out a type treatment that complemented it. As the image that was supplied was a collage, I wanted to make sure that the typeface really cut through and packed a punch." A double gatefold wallet has been used together with a poster insert, and VMR typeface has been used throughout.

OUT **IN**

A Bugged Out Mix by Klaxons

01/ Luke Vibert – Breakbeat Metal Music
02/ The L Bit – Tasty
03/ Pedro Campos – Butterfly
04/ Markus Lange & Daniel Dexter –
Shooting Tigers (Play Paul Remix)
05/ Johannes Heil – Artology
06/ Overnoise – Dry
07/ Blende – Breaking Bones
08/ Friendly – Ride Baby Ride (Strip Mix)
09/ Da BoogieBoys – Audiotonique
10/ The Chemical Brothers – It Doesn't Matter
11/ Justice – Stress
12/ Mogg & Naudascher – Moon Unit Part 1
13/ Klaxons – It's Not Over Yet (Brodinski Remix)
With Aleister Crowley – 666

A Bugged In Selection by Klaxons

01/ Zager & Evans – In The Year 2525
02/ Wu-Tang Clan – Shame On A Nigga
03/ Fad Gadget – King Of The Flies
04/ Liars – They Don't Want Your Corn,
They Want Your Kids
05/ United States Of America –
The Garden Of Earthly Delights
06/ Josef K – Sorry For Laughing
07/ Frankie Lymon & The Teenagers –
I'm Not A Juvenile Delinquent 'Rock, Rock, Rock'
08/ Todd Rundgren – Zen Archer
09/ Frankie Valli And The Four Seasons – The Night
10/ Cluster – Caramel
11/ Ariel Pink's Haunted Graffiti – For Kate I Wait
12/ Blur – Me, White Noise
13/ 90 Day Men – We Blame Chicago
14/ Roy Orbison – It's Over

Product: CD
Client/Label: New State
Artist: Various
Design: Richard Robinson
Collage: Jamie Reynolds
Country: UK

Folk Songs for the Five Points

This CD is the audio artifact of a project recording contemporary immigrant experiences in New York. Gunn, a British immigrant, collected found sound from the "Five Points" area in Lower Manhattan where many cultures, groups, and clashing socioeconomic groups still cross paths. The idea was for these experiences to be interpreted aurally; an audio journey through the streets of the Lower East Side. Joe Marianek designed the packaging. "Since the music is an abstract layering and interweaving of multiple voices and physical places, which are at times unsettling, I figured that a mix of disorienting things like mazes and moiré patterns would get at that," he explains. "All of the abstract lines have to do with place—separation, inclusion, and movement—and the geometric lettering and points illuminate the title *Five Points*."

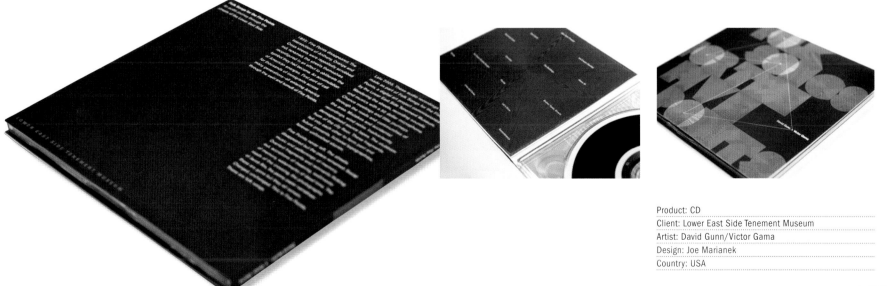

Product: CD
Client: Lower East Side Tenement Museum
Artist: David Gunn/Victor Gama
Design: Joe Marianek
Country: USA

Artwork

Defected Presents
Charles Webster

This CD and vinyl release features a mix of Webster's own tracks together with those of other artists. "One stipulation of the brief was that Webster wanted to appear on the artwork, but did not want to be the focal point, hence his appearance on the laptop screen. Surrounding the laptop is an imaginary world of color and shapes which emanates from pieces of studio equipment that he uses to create his tracks. Wired into the image is a girl relaxing and listening to the music." Peter Chadwick devised the image concept, then commissioned Manel to create it. Avant Garde Extra Light and Book typeface was used throughout the package.

Product: CD/Vinyl
Client/Label: Defected
Artist: Charles Webster
Design: Popular
Illustration: Stephane Manel/Debut Art
Country: UK

Defected: In the House

This was quite a large set of releases and they all needed to tie together somehow. "I created the illustrations in a circular shape with a central face on each. This central face stayed constant through all of the illustrations on the different releases to hold them together as a set," explains designer Steven Wilson.

Product: CD/Vinyl
Client/Label: Defected Records
Artist: Various
Design: Zip Design
Illustration: Steven Wilson
Country: UK

A Tale of 2 Cities

The packaging for this album was art directed by
Paul West and designed by West with assistance
from Becky Johnson, Andy Harvey, and Arran
Lidgett from design agency Form. "The album
cover was a painting by Clara Drummond, who
was commissioned by Mr Hudson," explains
West. "We worked closely with Mr Hudson and
Clara, photographing the sides and back of the
canvas to create a complete album package."
Inside the packaging, the songs' diverse subjects
and lyrics were interpreted as different book
layouts and designs.

Product: Vinyl
Client/Label: Mercury Records
Artist: Mr Hudson & The Library
Art Direction: Paul West
Design: Form
Painting: Clara Drummond
Country: UK

Artwork

Tourist/Half Light/Wires

Reflecting the sentiments of the album title, the images that Big Active have created for *Tourist* suggest a metaphorical journey to a series of destinations based around ideas and interpretations from the band's cryptic and idiosyncratic lyrics. "We chose five tracks to work with including the tracks which would eventually be used to promote the album as singles," explains Gerard Saint. "Working with the artist and set stylist Lyndsay Milne, we created a series of 'junk sculptures' using found objects held together with wires, tapes, and all manner of binding materials connected to form a vast installation—which unified the piece and provided a visual route from one destination to another—much the same as each song was sequenced on the album itself." The installation was then photographed as a series of high-production still life's by Dan Tobin Smith to give each the sense of placement in a vast space. The designers then created the album booklet using a long "roll-fold" format which opens out from the cover to reveal the complete installation. For the singles, various destinations were isolated to form specific cover images and support material for the album campaign.

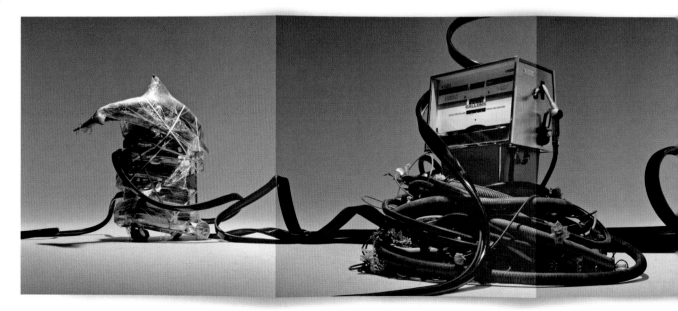

ATHLETE
WIRES

ATHLETE
TOURIST

Product: CD/Vinyl
Client/Label: Parlophone Recordings
Artist: Athlete
Art Direction: Richard Andrews/Gerard Saint/
Big Active
Design: Big Active
Photography: Dan Tobin Smith
Set Design: Lyndsay Milne
Country: UK

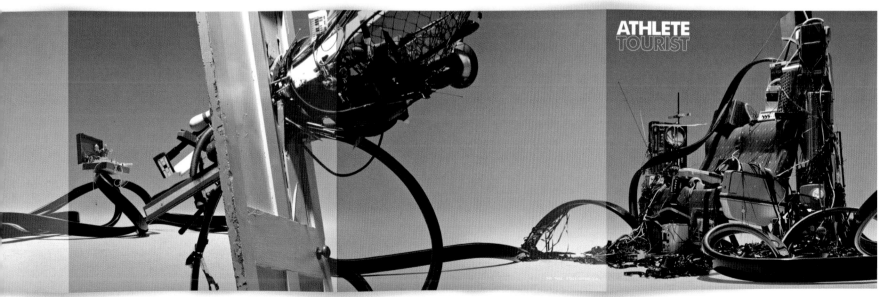

ATHLETE
TOURIST

Typography

Eco

"We wanted the cover artwork to be abstract, but at the same time communicate a feel of digital or electronic music," explains designer Flavio Bagioli. "The shape we have created resembles the letters S and K (the first two letters of Skipsapiens), but it's pretty free for any interpretation really. The other idea is that the layering effect of the graphics relates to the layered nature of the music, which is very common now in making electronic music." Bagioli created the graphic using a pixel-stretching technique with different color combinations to resemble harmonies and layers of sound. "I guess I looked for color combinations and the musicians looked for sound combinations or harmonies, so it's like groups of harmonies on the cover." The track listings were laid out by designers at Mutek Records, following the template it uses for all of its releases.

Product: CD
Client/Label: Mutek Records
Artist: Pier Bucci/Daniel Nieto/Skipsapiens
Design: Flavio Bagioli
Countries: Canada/Chile

Typography

Love Attack

Love Attack is Skatebård's second 12in release. The visual expression is a continuation of that used for his debut album *Midnight Magic* (see page 077). However, in contrast to his previous album's artwork, which was heavily influenced by 1980s horror movies and heavy metal, this artwork is more minimal with darker imagery. This reflects and contrasts with the music and content, with its warm title and electronic sound.

Product:	Vinyl
Client/Label:	Kompakt Records
Artist:	Skatebård
Design:	Grandpeople
Country:	Norway

Vivid

"After hearing the name of the artist, we kept thinking about organs, both man-made and organic ones, so we created a composite image using this imagery," explains designer Ariel Aguilera. "The idea was to represent the music as a living form created both by man and machine. The artist also requested to have a taste of hip-hop in the cover, as his music contains elements of the genre. We decided to use the image of an arrow to address this, as it is a commonly used element in graffiti and it also gave the whole design a sense of movement. All these 'living' concepts also tied in nicely with the title and the nature of the music." The basic idea for the package was to make the typographic layout part of the image and not a separate element. The package imagery came from photographs of old organ keyboards and medical organ illustrations that Pandarosa has collected.

Product: CD
Client/Label: AKA Ltd.
Artist: ORGA
Design: Pandarosa
Countries: Australia/Japan

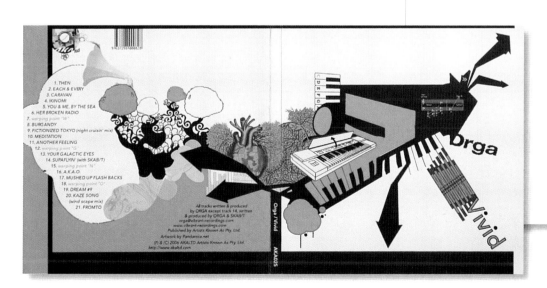

Typography

Tokyo Disko/Especial/
Piece Together

Chris Bolton designed this series of record covers. "The sleeve design comes directly from either the title of the group or the title track," explains Bolton. "For the arrow design of the typeface, I used Avant Garde as a base and chose it for its good geometric shapes from which I could build the basic letters." The placement of the lettering on the cover is because the group's name Reverso 68 adds up to nine characters and works well as three in a row, so Bolton created a simple three by three grid. "On the back of the sleeve, I wanted something more free, so seemingly random lines of text have been placed in the space all linked together with arrowed lines," he adds. The sleeves have been printed on uncoated stock.

Product: Vinyl
Client/Label: Eskimo Recordings/N.E.W.S.
Artist: Reverso 68
Design: Chris Bolton
Countries: Belgium/Finland

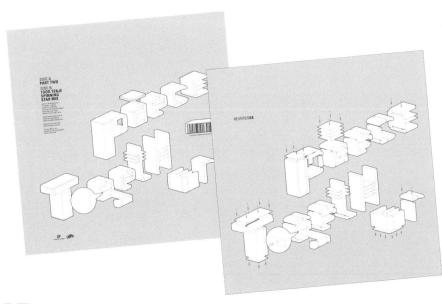

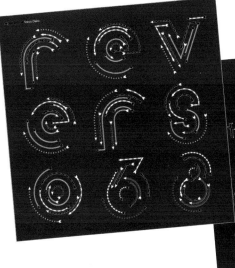

Ooh Aah

The Sweptaways, a choir of 30 women, performs a cappella cover versions of songs by artists such as Jenny Wilson, Pet Shop Boys, Kiss, Black Sabbath, and Kate Bush. Tyra von Zweigbergk designed this packaging for its debut album, *Ooh Aah*, and single, *Wuthering Heights*. "The Sweptaways has a lot to do with the costumes," she explains. "It is about elegance, fun, to be however one wants, and glamor… the simple necklace on the cover on the background of a skin tone was for me a nice way to zoom in and go past all the bright colors and big dresses; it became intimate." Inside the CD booklet is a photomontage of the choir members. The main typefaces used on the CD covers were designed by von Zweigbergk.

Product: CD
Client/Label: Hybris
Artist: The Sweptaways
Design: Tyra von Zweigbergk
Illustration: Tyra von Zweigbergk
Photography: Thomas Klementsson
Country: Sweden

OOH AAH

I WANT YOU
LET MY SHOES LEAD ME FORWARD
WUTHERING HEIGHTS
CHANGES
KALLA MIG
GO WEST
IT NEVER ENTERED MY MIND
VINTERSAGA
YOU DON'T OWN ME
SAY

DIRECTED BY SOPHIE EKLÖF

AGNES LUNDSTRÖM
EMMA GÖTHNER
SAMIRA BOUABANA
ASTRID STENBERG
JOSEFIN LUNDSTRÖM
EVA CLASING
SARA TELEMAN
FRIDA KOČI
KARINA FALK
LOTTA LANNEBO

PERNILLA SÖDERBERG
PAULA LUNDIN
MAINA ARVAS
JENNY SKOGH
MALIN SAHLSTEDT
ELLEN VON ZWEIGBERGK
TYRA VON ZWEIGBERGK
ÅSA ANESÄTER
ANNIKA BERG
MALIN MARMGREN
IKA JOHANNESSON
JOHANNA JARMEUS
KARIN BOHLIN
ANNA BÄFVERFELDT
INGRID UNSÖLD
CLARA GUSTAFSSON
ERICA JACOBSON

Jealous Girls

David Lane designed the branded packaging for all formats of this single and its promotional material. Each format featured a different video still, photographed on set by Tanna. "I felt that the imagery from the video, namely the band peeking out from behind venetian blinds, represented the idea of the song as well as anything," explains Lane. "The stills were cropped and placed to get maximum effect on each format and the fact that no shoot had to be arranged meant there was budget to print different images on each of the formats." Lane designed a custom title type for the single, and used Amasis for the label copy and credits.

Product: CD/Vinyl
Client/Label: Back Yard Recordings
Artist: Gossip
Design: David Lane
Photography: Shamil Tanna
Video Direction: Ollie Evans
Country: UK

Click

Ricky Tillblad designed this package for the
release of the 12in vinyl single *Click*. "The track
is called *Click*, so I thought, why not include
a camera on the sleeve?" explains Tillblad. "It is
an absolute no-no to be obvious within the field
of graphic design, but I decided to ignore that."
Tillblad used a camera image complemented
with a retro-looking typeface for the word "click."
"I stretched parts of the text 'click' to make it
feel a bit technical, or a bit like a barcode," he
explains. "I have then used colored gradients in
the lines that run above and below it." All other
cover text is set in Helvetica.

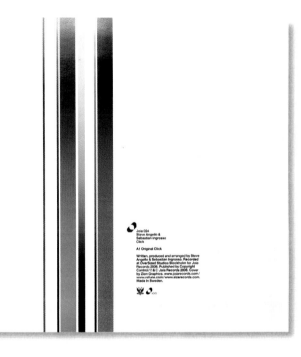

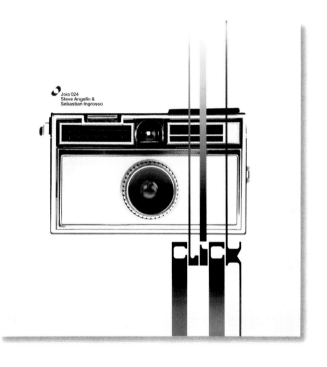

Product:	Vinyl
Client/Label:	Joia Records
Artist:	Steve Angello/Sebastian Ingrosso
Design:	Zion Graphics
Country:	Sweden

Laceration

Christian Hundertmark designed the package for this CD with the brief that the album title *Laceration*, hip-hop slang for lacing, should be visible within the artwork. "The design solution was to build a typographic layout, which was designed around the outlines of sneakers," he explains. "The words featured on the cover have been taken from the choruses of some of the songs on the album." This innovative solution to typographic layout was set using the classic typeface Helvetica.

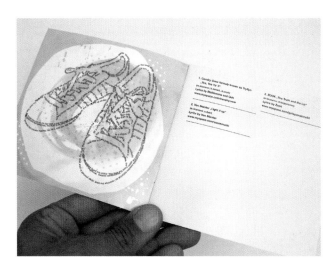

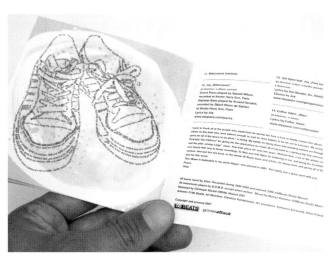

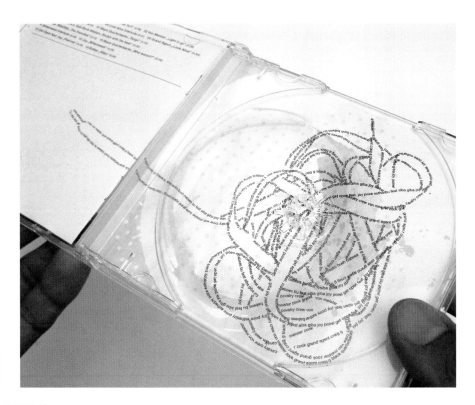

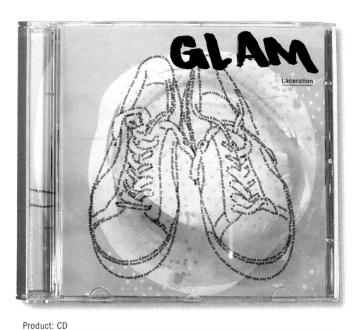

Product: CD
Client/Label: 58 Beats
Artist: Glam
Design: C100 Studio
Country: Germany

Petals on a Wet Black Bough

David Bailey created the cover for the release of this three-track EP CD with the name of the artist as a predominant feature on the front, together with several appropriate illustrations. "Lyrics from songs and sounds influenced the choice of colors and imagery that I used," explains Bailey. "The general vibe of the songs helped influence the media used, the colors, pencils, paints, and inks... most of the artwork was made while listening to the artist's music." Bailey created the front cover typography from an existing font in *Art Deco Alphabets*. This old movie-theater lettering suits the music and provides a focus on the front cover. The writing on the back is hand lettering; Bailey wanted simple lettering that would not intrude on the imagery shown above it. Interestingly, Bailey printed the covers on an Epson stylus color 1160 printer, and the stock used varied from pale yellow thin card to heavy off-white recycled paper. "I chose stock the ink would sit well on, with a slight variation in papers to make the covers more individual," adds Bailey.

Product: CD
Client/Artist: Petals on a Wet Black Bough
(aka David Roocroft)
Design: David Bailey
Country: UK

Typography

The Thing That Wears My Ring

Richard Niessen designed this CD package with the brief to create something "wild," as the band had described its music as being like a children's playground falling on your head. "I hand drew a special Scram C Baby font, inspired by the word 'playground,'" explains Niessen, "and based the design around that typeface throughout the booklet and on the disc." He has set other text in Futura. The package was produced as a limited edition of 1,000.

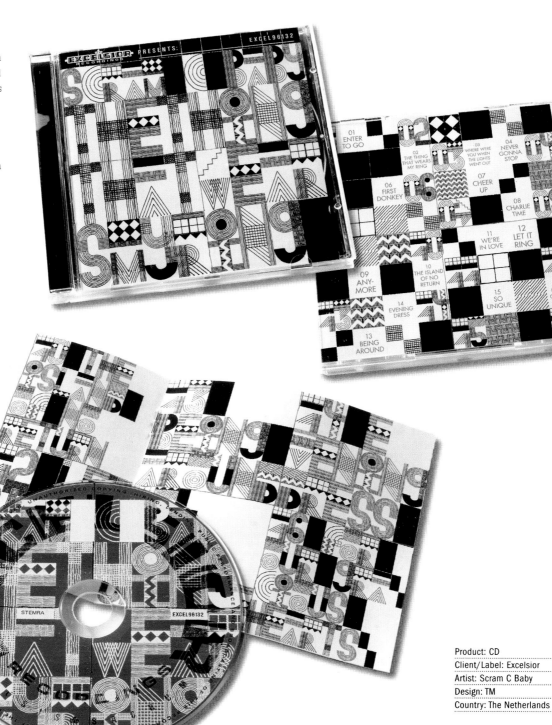

Product: CD
Client/Label: Excelsior
Artist: Scram C Baby
Design: TM
Country: The Netherlands

Grote Kunst Voor Kleine Mensen

Richard Niessen and Esther de Vries created the artwork for this children's DVD packaging together with the DVD menus. Their brief was to design a world through which the viewer could navigate, and their square-based design solution runs across both the physical packaging and the digital menus. "We designed a very graphical world, which was hand drawn to contrast to the short films on the DVD," explains Niessen. "We built it out of squares so that, as animation amateurs, we could easily animate it." Memphis typeface has been used to sit inside the hand-drawn squares. The six-panel DVD digipak was produced in a limited run of 1,500.

Product: DVD
Client: Cut-n-Paste
Design: TM
Country: The Netherlands

Typography

147

Fatos e Notas

Helio Zanepe designed this CD cover for Brazilian hip-hop band Nucleo's debut album (*Facts and Notes*). "We decided to base the design on newspaper design, but give it a different angle by giving it some additional info that looks like it was made by hand with a red pen," explains Zanepe. This has been done by adding what appear to be doodles on the cover and someone filling out a Word Search on the back, which relates to the track listings.

Product: CD
Client/Artist: Nucleo
Design: TELA.TV
Country: Brazil

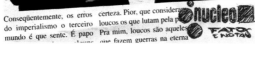

Take A Picture

This 12in features five tracks by 3-1 whose music is best described as electropunk, pistol pop. "There was no real briefing for the project," explains Ivo Schmetz. "As 310k does all the design for Basserk and has complete freedom to do what we like, it is always a matter of listening to the music and finding a good visual way to fit the tracks." The artwork has been created based on the EP's title with the cover image featuring the band members all with cameras in a collage. The hand-drawn text for the cover fits well with the other design that 3-1 uses on its website and in its videos. The other collage elements are taken from the different countries where 3-1 has done live shows. All other text has been set in Helvetica.

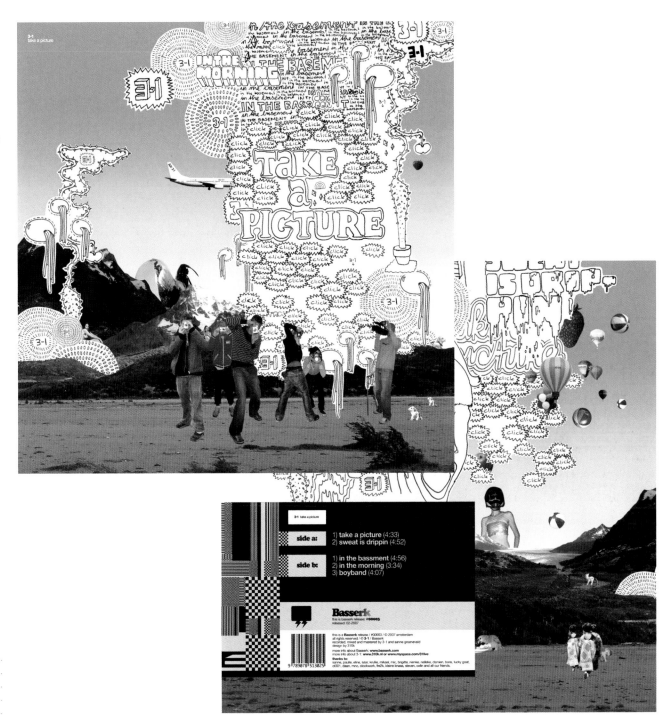

Product: Vinyl
Client/Label: Basserk
Artist: 3-1
Design: 310k
Country: The Netherlands

Slow Club

For this CD package, pleaseletmedesign created a "slow club," and also experimented with typography using the bodies of the band. The package cover features a scene from the "slow club," which has been created using cut-out imagery, photographed by Cornil, and collage. Inside, the package folds out to reveal the band's name, which has been spelt out using silhouette images of the band members, photographed by Cornil. ITC Caslon and ITC Lubalin typefaces have been used throughout.

Product: CD
Client/Label: 62TV
Artist: Flexa Lyndo
Design: pleaseletmedesign
Photography: Olivier Cornil
Country: Belgium

Returned no 01/
Returned no 03

The Returned series consists of three 12in discs with edits of tracks that were originally released in the mid-1990s. In its cover designs, desres design group overprinted the original release date with the newer release date. Chalet Paris Nineteen Sixty typeface has been used for the track listing with a modified VSV-Melon used for the title face.

Product: Vinyl
Client: Ian Pooley
Label: Freibank Musikverlage (GEMA)
Design: desres design group
Country: Germany

Influenza B

Vår designed this cover, which was inspired by the title of one of the tracks—*Dirty Needles*—in the release. "We wanted to interpret the title literally to make it interesting," explains Karl Grandin. "Of course it refers to intravenous drug use, but it could also be about sewing or knitting. We thought it might be interesting to see it as a mix." All cover artwork was drawn by hand, as was the text that is an extension of the main imagery. Other cover text has been set in Akzidenz. The package has been printed on a sleeve that has been turned inside out so that the cover is rough and uncoated and the inside smooth.

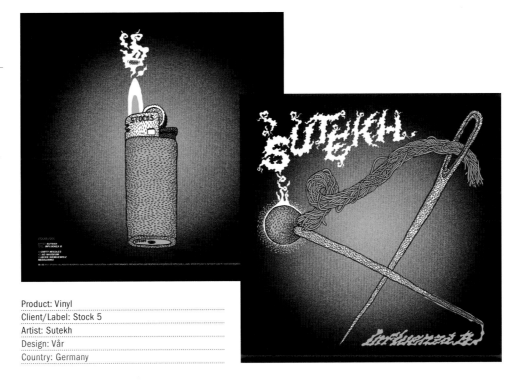

Product: Vinyl
Client/Label: Stock 5
Artist: Sutekh
Design: Vår
Country: Germany

Animationsafgangsfilm

This DVD features six movies that are diploma assignments of animation directors. The main idea behind the design was to create imagery using hand-drawn letters that also spell out the DVD title on the cover. The concept then continues through the rest of the package, with the lines appearing in different ways and different colors on all aspects of the packaging, from the DVD to the booklet.

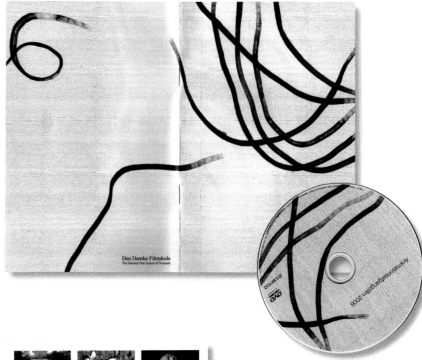

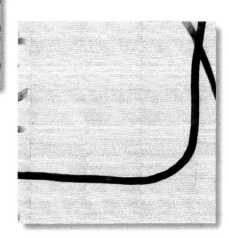

Product: DVD

Client: National Film School of Denmark

Design: Jan Oksbøl Callesen/Gul Stue/
Torsten Høgh Rasmussen

Country: Denmark

Let's Lazertag Sometime

The idea behind this typographic design was to feature a list of all the bands on the cover to show that the album was a compilation. A specially designed typeface was created for the cover. The inside of the package features illustrations showing several beings playing lazertag in a surrealistic landscape, in reference to the album title. On top of that, various media—photography, pen, paint, vector graphics, and collage—were used to show that the CD contains different music styles from different artists.

Product: CD
Client/Label: Tigerbeat6
Artist: Various
Design: Nathanaël Hamon/Slang/Wiyumi/
Jaana Davidjants
Country: USA

Surround Cuts

Nicole Jacek and Jan Wilker designed this DVD package for German jazz bassist Hellmut Hattler. They were responsible for creating not only the DVD packaging, but also the user interface on the DVD and a promotional poster for its release. "The idea for the design of the package and all the other elements surrounding the DVD was to take the songs and transform them into a space-like mutating fantasy 3D object without using any 3D software," explains Jacek. "We made a 3D object out of the song titles, transformed it in Illustrator, and used this as the starting point for the visual. We then further played around until we got our final object." FF DIN typeface was used; however, there are only single fragments on the cover, because the designers destructed the typeface for the visuals.

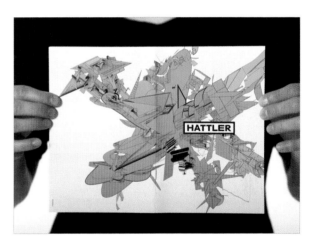

Product: DVD
Client/Label: Bassball Recordings
Artist: Hellmut Hattler
Design: Karlssonwilker Inc.
Country: USA

28 After

Non-Format designed this cover with an open brief which asked only that they reflect the nature of the music within the packaging. "We have been working with the photographer Jake Walters for many years and the image on this cover came out of an image test session we worked on with him," explains Jon Forss. "The black painted lips were manipulated in Photoshop to make them as iconic and impactful as possible. To this we added typography using a typeface we produced especially for the project. We wanted the overall effect to be as simple and strong as possible and also to have a dark edge that would reflect the sinister sound of the name Black Devil Disco Club." Non-Format created Uffda (the primary typeface) and Uffda Lite for the album title; the supporting type is set in Avant Garde. The type wraps over onto the back of the sleeve to suggest an automated design process that is not quite perfect. The sleeve has been printed on the reverse, uncoated side of the board for added tactility.

LUX

Marc Antosch was given just one week to design the packaging for this debut CD. "It had to be something simple because of the short deadline," he explains. "I wanted something big and bold so I played around with the three letters (LUX) and tried different color combinations before deciding on the gradients and overlaps that can be seen on the cover." The typographic design has been carried through to the CD itself, which also features the word LUX, although in different color gradients. The result is a package that has real impact despite its simple, minimal design.

Product: Vinyl
Client/Label: Lo Recordings
Artist: Black Devil Disco Club
Design: Non-Format
Photography: Jake Walters/Non-Format
Countries: UK/USA

Product: CD
Client/Label: LUX
Artist: LUX
Design: Tilt Design Studio
Country: Germany

Sampler Part 2

This vinyl release showcases four experimental techno tracks. Andreas Emenius designed the package keeping in tune with the label's feeling of warm techno, yet making something different. "The idea was to make a paradoxical image consisting of organic shapes and geometric figures," explains Emenius. "It was inspired by the music, which is fairly monotone with a warm atmosphere. The organic figures were chosen because they were neither hand drawn nor completely computer generated, but a sort of in-between, and slightly generic, which gave a good rough feeling that related to the music."

Product: Vinyl
Client/Label: Tangent Beats
Artist: Ronin/David Panda/Mille/Juho Kahilainen
Design: Andreas Emenius
Country: Sweden

Typography

1000 Beats/1 Beat

Ginckels collaborated with producer Cristian Vogel and Grandpeople to make the vinyl record shown here. The idea of the arts project was to create a record that would form part of a touring exhibition in Europe. Visitors to the exhibition then had the chance to play the record on several turntables at the same time, at different speeds, creating different DJ sets and controlling the music. The brief was to make something "object-like" and not a regular record cover. "The design is very simple—image on one side, and text on the other," explains Magnus Voll Mathiassen. "This was to keep the 'object-like' feeling Ginckels wanted to have with it stripped down to the essentials." The diamond alludes to the turntable's stylus, referring to the action of playing a record. Grandpeople created the ornate, highly detailed typeface used. The vinyl was printed as a limited run of 1,000.

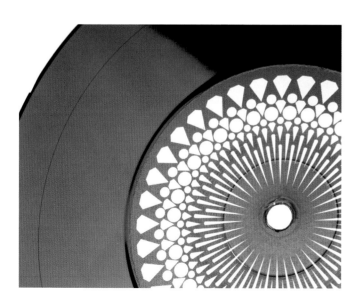

Product: Vinyl
Client: Pieterjan Ginckels
Design: Grandpeople
Countries: Belgium/Norway

My Occupation

Richard Robinson's design of this CD package
for Chaz Jankel (formerly of The Blockheads)
revolves around a reworked version of an Albert
Hollenstein typeface. "I loved the fact that
it looked really modern, but was designed over
20 years ago," explains Robinson, "much in the
same way that a lot of the tracks on the album
are." He restricted himself to just two colors,
partly so he could use two strong Pantones as
opposed to CMYK, and partly because he thought
it would give the package more in-store impact.
The inside of the package features a stripped
back version of the type, which looks abstract,
but in fact spells out CHAZ. Despite the limited
budget, Robinson secured the use of heavier
weight stock and gloss finish.

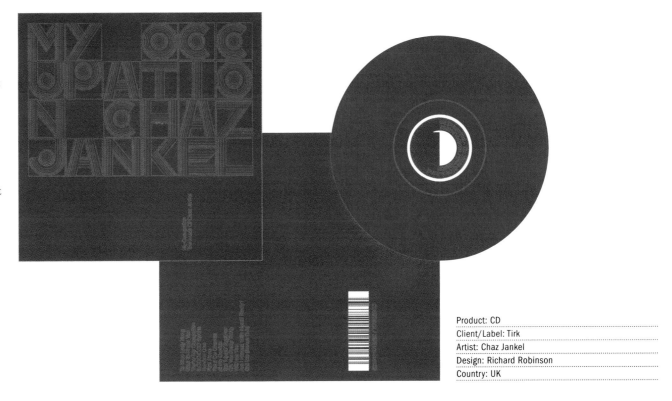

Product: CD
Client/Label: Tirk
Artist: Chaz Jankel
Design: Richard Robinson
Country: UK

Ricky Tillblad
Zion Graphics
Sweden

When designing packages for CDs, vinyl, or DVDs what inspires you?
It can be a lot of different things. Everything from a bassline to a great color combination, but in most cases the biggest inspiration is the artist. Sometimes the title of the CD gives the inspiration.

What do you most enjoy about working on these projects?
I enjoy seeing a seed of an idea growing into a great artwork and marketing tool.

Who has been your best client/artist to work with?
One of my best is the singer in the band The Ark. He is so inspiring to work with, and also interested in design and art. We both have strong ideas so it can be a real struggle to work for The Ark, but it always pushes the project further.

What is the most important function for a cover, or package, to perform?
Of course the packaging should reflect the music and the artist, but it should also be visibly strong so it will catch your eye in the store. Nowadays it also has to work in really small formats, in MP3 stores such as iTunes. I think The Ark's *State of The Ark* is an example of a cover with strong shapes and simple graphics that makes you interested in the album. Another example is The Ark's single *The Worrying Kind*, which also has strong graphics making it really stand out in a small format.

What is your favorite CD or vinyl package of all time?
My favorite vinyl cover is Peter Saville's for New Order's *Power, Corruption & Lies*. I like the way he uses an old painting of flowers and makes it feel contemporary. My favorite CD cover is Tiken Jah Fakoly's *Françafrique*. The image of the artist on an old moped is cool and gives the right feel to this album.

What do you think the future holds for music and movie packaging now that so much music (and soon movies) can be downloaded, and how do you think the role of the graphic designer might change because of this?
I think the role of graphic designers will be more one of a designer for the group/ artist rather than a designer for a specific album. I think it will be more important to make a coherent concept for websites, covers, merchandise, images, etc.

What can designers do to move with the "digital times" and offer buyers something other than simply a thumbnail image of an album cover when they download music?
I think that they could create a combination of animations and graphic design, making moving images to give away with the downloaded files.

Jon Tye
Lo Recordings/LoAF/LoEB
UK

What is the most important function for a cover/package to perform?
For me the cover must express the feeling of the music, but also create a certain sense of mystery. It should have an almost sensual quality. The sleeve for *Milky Disco* is a perfect example because it transmits images of space, planets, and breasts (milk)... the shapes in the font are very feminine and even mystical—disco for me has a strong feminine vibe unlike happy hardcore or drum and bass and because of the more "cosmic" nature of some of the music, there is a mystical element—the overall effect is also fresh and new, perfect for a new cosmic disco selection. The Black Devil Disco Club's *28 After* sleeve is great because it is dark like the music and mysterious like the story of the Black Devil Disco Club—the true identity of Black Devil and the date when the music was recorded is still under discussion.

What is the most interesting piece of packaging you have come across in this area?
Probably the LoAF packaging because it doesn't conform to the usual format restrictions, and mixes materials and processes. I like the use of screen printing, which is very tactile, and that the board is much bigger than it needs to be to accommodate a 3in CD. Also, each release features a poster by a different artist, which creates a strong visual identity, but one that has an oblique relationship with the music. The first Vincent Oliver EP is great in that the illustration is recognizably Vincent, but it's a different world from the one he normally inhabits.

How do you approach the briefing of designers?
I like them to hear the music and sometimes we discuss the overall "feel" of the release, but I think with Non-Format, we have been working together long enough for them intuitively to know what we require.

Are decisions about covers/packages based on their marketability or their design aesthetic?
I think if the design aesthetic is strong then it is easy to market.

What do you think the future holds for music and movie packaging now that so much music (and soon movies) can be downloaded, and how do you think the role of the graphic designer might change because of this?
For me the CD was never a great format for visuals compared to vinyl and I think with downloads/iPod etc., they are rapidly becoming obsolete. I think the designer will have to become more part of the creative process—considering how the combination of music and visuals can affect the listener/consumer. The potential is there to have a far stronger effect; computers and laptops in particular already can make their owners feel quite attached to them. There is the possibility to truly envelop the listener in a world of sound and vision. As yet, however, there is only a fairly standard PDF digital booklet or just a JPEG of the sleeve illustration. I hope with our designers we can find some interesting new solutions to this problem.

What can designers do to move with the "digital times" and offer buyers something other than simply a thumbnail image of an album cover when they download music?
That's a good question. Wallpapers, screen savers, and slideshows all have potential, but in the same way that most design is lacking in originality and creativity, so most download art will be lacking. We need to find ways to make it exciting and stimulating.

Extending the Experience

03

As this chapter shows, in some cases the purchase of a music CD, DVD, or vinyl not only provides the user with a listening experience, but also can extend their experience and provide them with "added extras." Physically, there are many ways in which this is done, from the inclusion in a package of an unusually extensive book or booklet, to sheets of stickers. Digitally, the opportunities are also growing.

Designers now have the opportunity to create downloadable artwork. This can be made available to consumers when purchasing an album via MP3s, or a package can include links to secret websites.

Whether physical or digital, added extras are the artist's or client's opportunity to give their fans something more, either to reward them for their loyalty or to increase sales and compete in this highly competitive market.

Digital

Story Like A Scar

Maiko Kuzunishi designed and illustrated this album package. "When I began the project, I had a discussion with the band's leader, songwriter, and singer Matthew Pryor," he explains. "One of the things he mentioned was his growing love of Kansas, and this became the main inspiration behind the design… but also, as the album title suggests, each scar has a story to tell. The album was also in a way the artist's personal reflection of the past as he grew into the future and it was important to reflect this in the visual artwork of the album." Kuzunishi wanted the overall album imagery to have a sense of renewal, and has used imagery such as the sun shining through clouds and layers of burnt holes to illustrate this. As the package is opened, the viewer sees a landscape unfolding and coming together. The CD also contains a link to a secret website featuring audio and video content.

Product: CD
Client/Label: Vagrant Records
Artist: The New Amsterdams
Design/Illustration: Decoylab
Country: USA

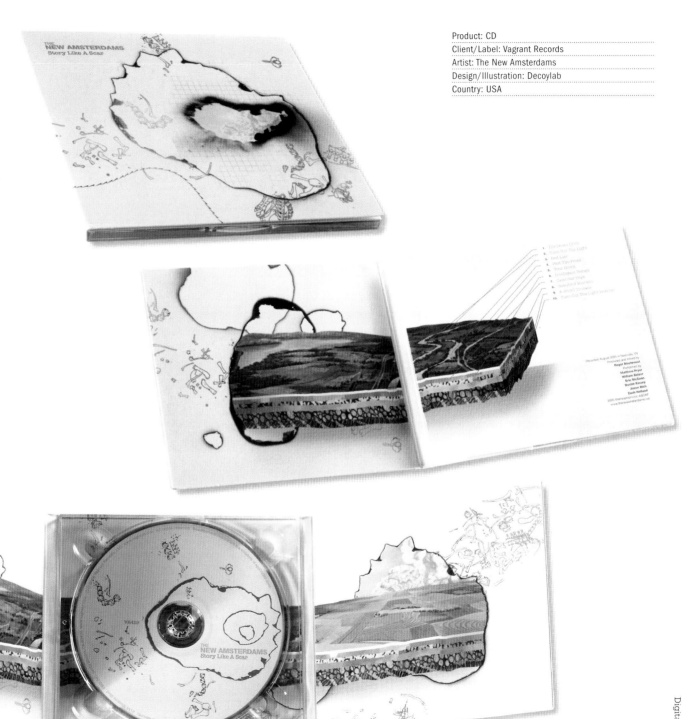

Public Transport

Julio Rölle created a cover for this online album, which features 11 tracks, and also a different "sub-cover" for each album track. "The design of the album cover and the subsequent tracks is deeply inspired by the music," explains Rölle. "When I designed it, I listened to the album at the same time… it is very deep, serious, and almost sad music about breaking hearts, love, and suicide." Rölle used just three colors (black, red, and white) within the design, which features a mix of photographs and hand-drawn, scribble-style typefaces. The album was also sold as a limited-edition custom-made cassette tape.

Product: CD
Client/Label: Kitty Yo Digital
Artist: The Tape vs. RQM
Design: Julio Rölle
Photography: Julio Rölle
Country: Germany

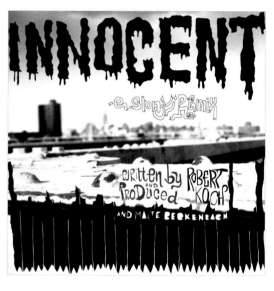

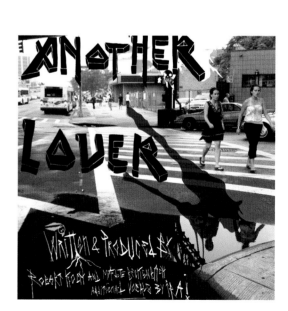

WRITTEN & PRODUCED BY ROBERT KOCH
Additional vocals by Sasha Perera

GunPlay

OUTRO

WRITTEN & PRODUCED BY ROBERT KOCH and FELLE P

ROBOTS CRY TOO!

PUBLIC TRANSPORT

WRITTEN AND PRODUCED BY ROBERT KOCH, ROMY AND MALTE BECKENBACH

WRITTEN AND PRODUCED ROBERT KOCH AND MALTE BECKENBACH

SEVEN HOURS!

ADDITIONAL VOCALS BY RA!

SIDE A. INNOCENT ALLOW

ANOTHER LOVER

OUTRO

SIDE B.

THE STATE vs. ROMY

GunPlay

PUBLIC TRANSPORT

ROBOTS CRY TOO!

SEVEN HOURS!

The World Is Yours

Joe Lewis created this digital interactive booklet, which was made available as part of a bundle when downloading the entire album using iTunes. Its design needed to be consistent with the physical album artwork so all images, fonts, etc., have been taken from that. It contains album lyrics, a photo gallery, and credits, along with a stencil image that can be downloaded and printed by the user. In addition, Lewis designed a straightforward, user-friendly menu to guide the user through the booklet.

Product: CD (e-book)
Client/Label: Polydor
Artist: Ian Brown
Design/Layout: Fury
Digital Design: Joe Lewis
Illustration: Ben Walsh
Photography: Lawrence Watson, Fabiola Quiroz-Brown, Shari Denson
Country: UK

The Drift

This digital booklet was released together with Scott Walker's first album in 11 years. Vaughan Oliver designed the physical album packaging, which Swinton then adapted to the digital booklet. The challenge was how to translate the original subtle, dark, intense physical album artwork into a "booklet" that could then be packaged with the digital release of the album through iTunes. Swinton had to embody the same spirit as the physical package within the digital one. This has been achieved well by including all the physical booklet's content—plus links to download desktops and a timeline about Walker—within the digital booklet.

Product: CD (digital booklet)
Client/Label: 4AD
Artist: Scott Walker
Design: v23
Digital Design: Graeme Swinton
Country: UK

We'll Live And Die In These Towns

Big Active designed this album packaging. "The album's title suggests sentiments of social dissatisfaction and a desire to escape the mundane existence of dead-end towns in search of something less predictable and more exciting," explains Gerard Saint. "Inspired by this sentiment, our cover visual focuses on the image of a ubiquitous railway departure board to boldly suggest escape or arrival… it conjures up feelings of municipal industry and nationalized dogma, as well as that of the routine pace of life running to an inevitable timetable." The design idea took the album track titles and used them in place of town/city names on the departure board on the album packaging. This design solution also provided Saint and his team with a device that could be effectively translated across many different formats and visual platforms throughout the campaign. This included static printed media, animated online media, digital downloads, live visuals, and TV advertising. For example, while the idea translates effectively as traditional packaging for the album, the visuals have also been animated as part of the bundled digital download. When a user purchases a digital version of the album and listens to it on an iPod, the track listings change on the iPod screen as they would on a train departure board. "We wanted to provide a complete album experience at all points of engagement with the music," adds Saint.

Product: CD (iPod graphics)
Client/Label: WEA Records
Artist: The Enemy
Art Direction: Gerard Saint/Big Active
Design: Big Active
Photography: Ben Weller/Big Active
Country: UK

17 Songs

Lucha Design created the packaging and digital element for this release of a collection of the most requested songs from the band's previous albums, as chosen by fans in a MySpace poll. The release was accompanied by a special website (www.17songs.com), where, among other features, the collage included in the booklet is translated into an interactive landscape, which relates various elements to the adventures of, and stories about, the band. "The idea for the design was simple and cheeky on the outside, a bit more dense on the inside," explains Agi Morawska. "Just like the music and the band itself. The five color lines reference the five members of the band and the five lines on music notation sheets, then a genuine 'just going for it' approach is behind the vinyl heart." A booklet enclosed in the CD package features a landscape which was collaged using graphics from Happy Pills' previous record covers, footage clips from videos, and elements that referenced a specific concert, interviews, etc. Continuing in the spirit of DIY, a four-panel horizontally unfolding booklet to present the landscape collage and a satin finish digipak are all the economical means used.

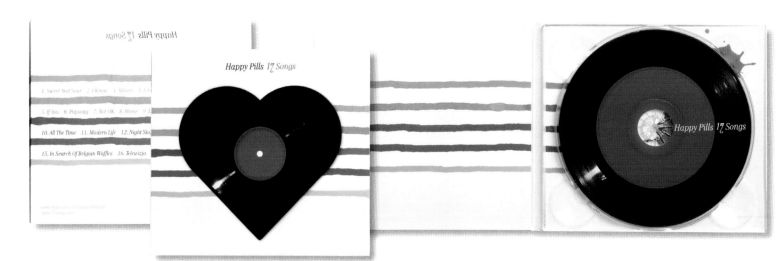

Product: CD
Client/Label: Antena Krzyku Unc.
Artist: Happy Pills
Design: Lucha Design
Photography: Jason Wyche
Country: USA

Digital

Overpowered/Let Me Know

Shown here are the promotional and commercial releases for *Overpowered* and *Let Me Know*. The concept for the sleeve designs, and for the campaign as a whole, centers on an image of Murphy as a "24-hour-a-day" pop star. "The idea was that she would always be in character, regardless of the banality of the situation," explains Scott King. "The thought that dictated the whole campaign was 'Ziggy Stardust in Wimpy Burger.'" I wanted her to appear 'beamed in' to our world from somewhere more incredible, like *The Man Who Fell To Earth*." Jonathan de Villiers photographed Murphy for the cover and subsequent single releases. Typography (set in Shelley Allegro Script) was kept to a minimum, confining it all to fluorescent stickers that were applied to the releases.

Product: CD/Vinyl (e-book)
Client/Label: EMI
Artist: Róisín Murphy
Design: Scott King
Photography: Jonathan de Villiers
Country: UK

1 LYRICS
THE WORLD IS YOURS ON TRACK   SISTER

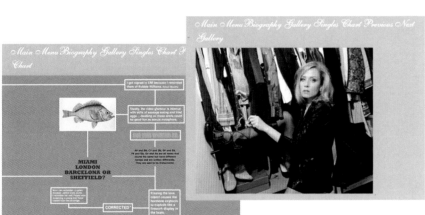

MIAMI
LONDON
BARCELONA OR
SHEFFIELD?

CORRECTED

Overpowered

RÓISÍN MURPHY

Album version
Instrumental

The Eraser

Shown here is the vinyl packaging release, which features Stanley Donwood's work, and the digital release that was created by Graeme Swinton. Donwood has a long association with Radiohead. This particular artwork, titled London Views, was created at the same time as the music on *The Eraser* album. However, at the time it was created, it was not necessarily going to be used as the album artwork—this decision came later. The artwork has also been adapted for use in a digital booklet that was produced to accompany the digital album on iTunes. The booklet has been produced in QuickTime using Flash, and not only adds value to the digital download, but also gives the user a witty, interactive way of scrolling across Donwood's London Views landscape while listening to the album.

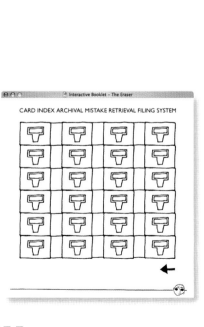

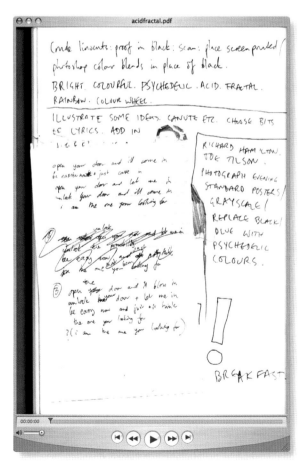

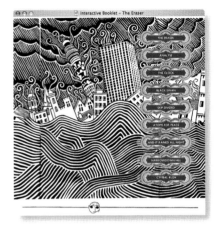

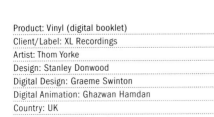

Product: Vinyl (digital booklet)
Client/Label: XL Recordings
Artist: Thom Yorke
Design: Stanley Donwood
Digital Design: Graeme Swinton
Digital Animation: Ghazwan Hamdan
Country: UK

Physical

Teach Dem

Oscar Wilson created the packaging for the release of this promotional 7in vinyl single featuring new solo material by Ashley Beedle (Warbox). "The idea was to produce something handmade, 'scratchy,' (not slick), and with possible slight variation from piece to piece," explains Wilson. "The combination of hand-screen printing with vacuum packing provided a solution." The single was manufactured in red vinyl with a white label and thin cardboard sleeve. The reggae-inspired record artwork was then screen printed (in three colors) simultaneously onto the sleeve and record label (through the sleeve's center hole). A complimentary three-color screen-printed T-shirt was also produced, and the record and T-shirt were vacuum packed together. The hand-drawn typography is based on Revue.

Product: Vinyl
Client: Gimme 5 UK Ltd.
Artist: Warbox
Design: Studio Oscar
Country: UK

Apoptygma Berzerk

Christian Hundertmark designed the package for this CD of remixes. "It evolved within several weeks," he explains. "The basic idea was that it should be a collage of different stuff, containing important elements that referred to the band's history. We used images we found in magazines, on the Internet, and also imagery we drew." For a limited-edition run, the package was printed as a "media book" (as shown here), which features a small book of imagery, lyrics, credits, etc. It was also produced in standard jewel case packaging. Hoefler typeface was used throughout.

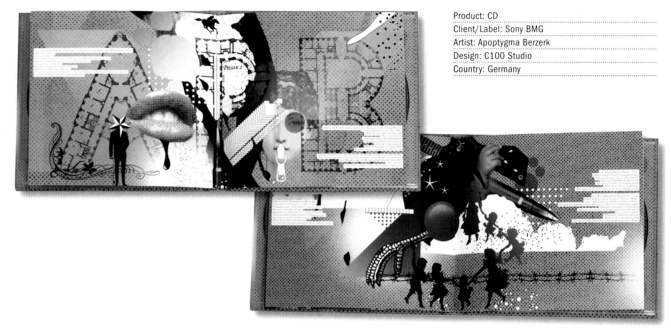

Product: CD
Client/Label: Sony BMG
Artist: Apoptygma Berzerk
Design: C100 Studio
Country: Germany

Moonless and Crowblack

This remix album was created from the Thread Pulls' *Fluorescent 3* album (see page 184). Only 50 copies were released, each one housed in a custom-made cardboard sleeve designed by Peter Maybury and accompanied by two large-format offset-lithographic prints that he also created. The posters were printed in one color onto white stock, while the sleeves were inkjet printed, hand-cut, and then folded. The catalog number on the CD was a custom-made rubdown transfer. Braggadocio, Bureau Grotesque, and Min Four typefaces have been used throughout. "I chose Braggadocio for the way it relates to the hexagon graphic and Bureau Grotesque for its blackness," explains Maybury.

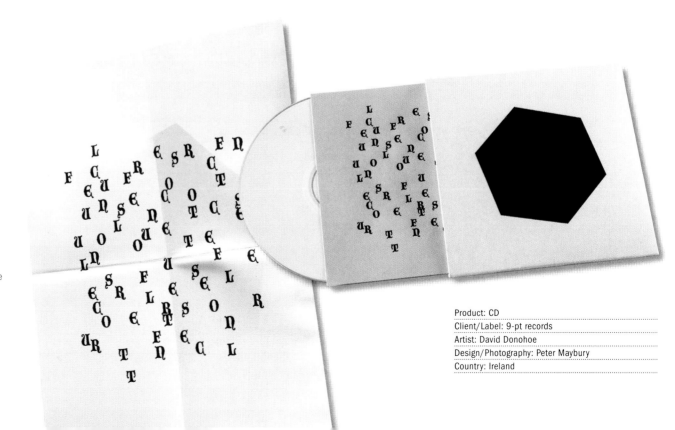

Product: CD
Client/Label: 9-pt records
Artist: David Donohoe
Design/Photography: Peter Maybury
Country: Ireland

Wildness & Trees

"The band bought the image after they saw it in a newspaper and insisted we use it on the cover," explains Damien Aresta. "We like challenges so it was a deal." The result is this CD package with the photograph on the cover. Inside, however, pleaseletmedesign was inspired by both the image and album title to create some map-like illustrations featuring silhouettes of the men in the photograph. This illustration has been made into a poster that was folded and inserted into the digipak package. Akzidenz Grotesk typeface has been used throughout.

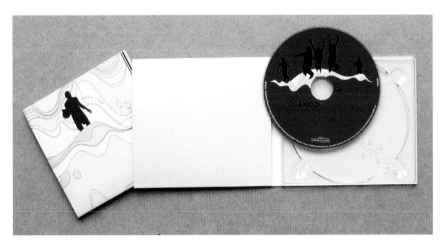

Product: CD
Client/Label: Soundstation
Artist: Superlux
Design: pleaseletmedesign
Photography: © AFP
Country: Belgium

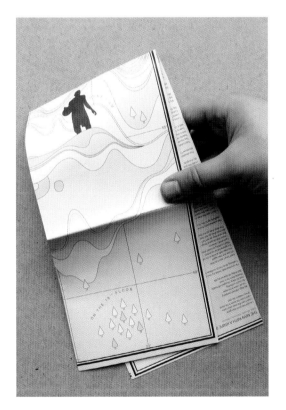

The Pipettes singles box set

Pete Hellicar created this set of 7in vinyl sleeves
to fit together in much the same way as the 7in
covers of the 1950s and 1960s. "The design for
the covers was inspired by the type of records
you would find in a girl's bedroom collection,"
explains Hellicar. "I looked at early covers from
the birth of pop and created a mix of hand-
drawn and generic imagery. I redrew a selection
of back designs that showed fake offers for
hairdryers and band photos that fitted with the
ideas we were working with." Hellicar has used
a mixture of rather mismatched type, which
looks wrong, but makes the sleeves more
authentic to the 1950s–1960s era. In addition,
the sleeves were made with poor-quality paper,
which adds to the feel of the product, and
printing was simple two-color litho. However,
the box in which the singles sit was printed
with gold ink and gloss laminated. Added extras
included Pipettes lollipops and stickers.

Product: Vinyl
Client/Label: Memphis Industries
Artist: The Pipettes
Design: Pete Hellicar
Country: UK

April & I

Paul Steel created the illustrations featured on both the 7in picture disc and the CD in this package. They narrate the naive tale of a boy, his imaginary friend, and the struggles of growing up. As the album is based on a child's tale, with childlike illustrations to match, the idea for the design of the CD package is taken from that of a children's board storybook. "Knowing the limited nature of the CD release, we wanted to make the packaging very special and utilize it to complete the storytelling concept of the album," explains Keith Davey. "The label wanted to do this to make impact as they introduced their new artist to the media, press, and radio."

1. April's Theme
2. April
3. Worst Day
4. Take It Or Leave It
5. School Bully
6. I Gave Her My Number
7. Honkin' (On My Crackpipe)
8. Grown Up And Away
9. April & I
10. Imaginary

Product: CD/Vinyl
Client/Label: Ray Gun
Artist/Illustration: Paul Steel
Design: Keith Davey/Red Design
Country: UK

april & I

by
PAUL STEEL

april told me from now on everything would be ok!

i told her about the worst day of my life.

she taught me how to get girls

one night i went to sleep

turns out i'm the one who's imaginary...

...but i got into class A drugs

Fluorescent 1, Fluorescent 2, Fluorescent 3

This series of CDs is housed in traditional DVD packaging. Peter Maybury created the packages and invited Garrett Phelan to collaborate with him. "I asked him to produce unique drawings and Polaroid photographs in response to the music and elements of the lyrics, and in relation to his overall art practice," he explains. Each copy is unique: *Fluorescent 1*, has a marker drawing on Fabriano 5 paper; *Fluorescent 2*, a Polaroid photograph in a paper bag; and *Fluorescent 3*, a marker drawing on the disc and an additional photographic print. In addition, each package has a sleeve insert that has been made with a custom-made rubdown transfer on fluorescent paper. Courier New typeface has been used for the text on the insert together with Min Four, which has been used for the label ID and catalog numbers on the CDs.

Product: CD
Client/Label: 9-pt records
Artist: Thread Pulls
Design: Peter Maybury
Concept: Peter Maybury/Garrett Phelan
Artworks/Illustrations: Garrett Phelan
Photography: Marie-Pierre Richard
Country: Ireland

Sumosonic (Vols 33–43)

Sumosonic is a monthly music compilation curated and produced by Heavy.com, a video website. Shown here are volumes 33–43 of the collection created mainly for self-promotional use. The CDs are packaged with a Sumosonic collector's card and often bundled with an additional bonus DVD that contains music videos and interactive media. The design of each month's compilation aims to reflect the voice and edgy personality of Heavy.com, which targets an 18–34-year-old demographic. "The specific ideas associated with each *Sumosonic* vary each month," explains Stephen Spyropoulos. "The main consistency is that each month we aim to produce a high-quality piece of design that our audience can relate to."

Product: CD/DVD
Client: Heavy.com
Artist: Various
Design: Stephen Spyropoulos/Daniel Weise
Country: USA

No Love Lost

No Days Off created the packaging for this debut album and subsequent singles. "The Rifles have a strong link to classic UK bands like The Jam and Oasis," explains Patrick Duffy. "It was important for this idea of musical heritage to come across in the design of their sleeves without resorting to cliché, so our solution was to concentrate on bold letterpress typography across all elements of the campaign; we saw letterpress type as having the same mixture of roughness and tradition as the band themselves, and would help them stand out from the usual 'band portrait and title' approach." Each letter was printed several times, then scanned and positioned individually, to give the designers as much control and variation as possible. "The imagery on the sleeves is subtle, mainly simple icons drawn from the lyrics," designer Patrick Duffy explains. "We wanted the letterpress type to work as the imagery, and so our efforts were concentrated on trying to create as much drama from the letterforms as possible while still keeping everything legible and structured." For all other text Clarendon typeface was used for its chunky serifs and classic feel. Each 7in single release had an added extra: *Repeated Offender* contained a specially designed poster, *She's Got Standards* was released on pink vinyl, and *Peace & Quiet* had the song lyrics etched into the vinyl itself.

Product: CD/Vinyl
Client/Label: Red Ink/Sony BMG
Artist: The Rifles
Design: No Days Off
Country: UK

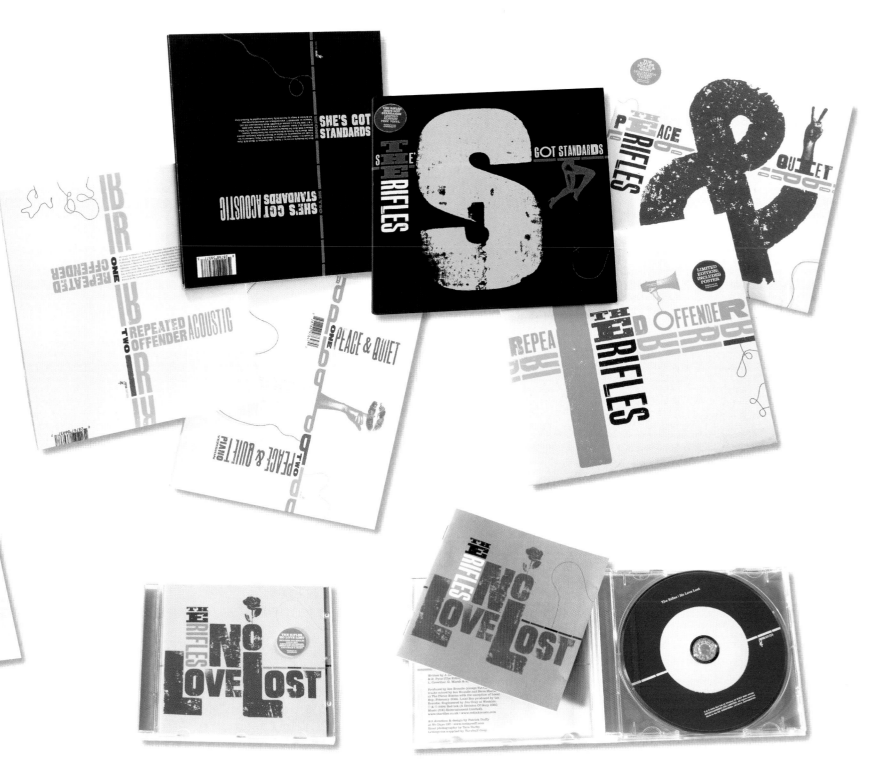

Thank You Dr. Martens

LOVE created this "thank you" box for shoe brand Dr. Martens to send to some of its key retailers. "With the traditional 1460 boot entering another cycle of popularity, they asked us to design a gift that could be sent out around the world," explain the designers at LOVE. "Our idea for the package design came from the music industry's gold disc award. With the close relationship between Dr. Martens boots and music, we thought a great way to reward the retailers was to give them a limited-edition yellow disc." Garamond, Helvetica, and Univers Bold Condensed typefaces all feature on the package. The vinyl contains a "baked" label, the black background features embossed gold foil, and the specially produced ultra-lightweight frame ensures low postage costs.

Product: Vinyl

Client: Dr. Martens

Design: LOVE

Country: UK

Our Love to Admire

This special limited-edition CD package includes a linen-bound book with the logotype foil stamped in black on the cover. "The band was very much involved in the creative process of the artwork," explains David Calderley. "They already had a very successful look which they wanted to get away from. The new concept was fairly established when I got involved: a shoot by Seth Smoot was done in the LA Museum of Natural History capturing what the band wanted from hundreds of detailed shots of the whole collection in the museum and used throughout the package." The limited version uses a black background together with black finishing and varnishes. It also features additional photographs and poster. Tiffany and Avant Garde typefaces are used with some hand-drawn elements.

Product: CD
Client/Label: Capitol
Artist: Interpol
Design: GraphicTherapy
Photography: Seth Smoot
Country: USA

Physical

Tala-Arawan

Inksurge created the packaging for this third album release. Tala-arawan means journal, or list of things to do, and it was this that provided the inspiration for the album cover design. "We wanted the package to look like the journal of a songwriter," explains Rex Advincula. "We asked the vocalist in the band to write the lyrics of each song on a blank sheet of paper together with some side-notes from the band, some scribbles and doodles in order to make it personal to them." Together with this, Inksurge has added Nicdao's photographs of the band. Centennial LT Roman typeface is used for its association with old notebooks and leather-bound books, and the cover also features a gold stamp.

Product: CD
Client/Label: EMI Philippines
Artist: Sugarfree
Design: Inksurge
Photography: Mark Nicdao
Country: Philippines

Five on the Floor

Having designed Sandwich's third album cover, Inksurge designed this fourth album cover and, given complete freedom with the design, asked simply to listen to the music and interpret it. "We are sticker addicts and so is the band," explains Rex Advincula. "At first it was three to four stickers for the album, but then we thought why not interpret each song title with a sticker, and we managed to get the band to approve this." The stickers feature in the album on a threefold sticker sheet and one sticker has been applied to the front of the jewel case to serve as a cover should the sticker sheet be completely removed. Coriander typeface was used for the package for its raw, hand-drawn feel.

Product: CD
Client/Label: EMI Philippines
Client/Artist: Sandwich
Design: Inksurge
Country: Philippines

R.E.M. Live

Chris Bilheimer designed this package, and although there was no brief, he wanted to use as little plastic as possible. "One of the most iconic images of this particular tour was Michael Stipe's wide stripe of blue eye makeup that went from ear to ear," explains Bilheimer. "At the end of an energetic performance, the makeup would have smeared, worn, and sweated off. Since that became a symbol of a great performance, a close-up of the distressed makeup seemed to sum up the live experience." An image shot by Belisle was used, and following the feel of the live performances, and the fact that the live video DVD in the package itself is distorted, Bilheimer wanted to use images on the remainder of the package that had been degraded by multiple layers of technology. Many of the images seen here are low-res screen grabs of video shot from a TV screen. Rocketship From Infinity typeface was used for the text on the package.

Product: CD
Client/Artist: R.E.M.
Design: Chris Bilheimer
Country: USA

R.E.M. fanclub holiday package

Every year the band R.E.M. send a package to every registered fanclub member to celebrate the year-end holidays. The band originally started the tradition in 1988 with a 7in vinyl record, and for the one shown here a four-track CD was included. Bilheimer designed the package. "The main objective was to create a really special keepsake for the fans that pay to be in the fanclub every year," he explains. "Since there are members in 40 countries, shipping has to be a big consideration, which is why the mailer envelope is part of the overall design. With so much international shipping to consider, the durability, weight, and costs are an important factor." So the package contains the CD in a die-cut cover, a sticker, and a calendar. All of the elements are printed black and gunmetal silver on the coated side, and four-color process on the uncoated side.

Product: CD/DVD
Client/Label: Warner Bros
Artist: R.E.M.
Design: Chris Bilheimer with Michael Stipe
Photography: David Belisle
Country: USA

Eddy Fresh

Kid Acne and Ben Weaver created this package for the release of the single *Eddy Fresh* from the album *Romance Ain't Dead*. The idea for the artwork, specifically the typography, stems from the album. "The typography was inspired by elements of Victorian theater posters and ephemera," explains Weaver. "The single also incorporates elements of Kid Acne's illustration and graffiti together with photographs which provide a contrast with the Victoriana elements of the album." The record cover shows Ashley's photographic portrait of Kid Acne, with a subtle reference to the single title, while the inner sleeve shows a Kid Acne drawing, together with Arbet's crude black-and-white snapshot. The package also includes a sticker sheet of brightly colored words taken from the single.

Product: Vinyl
Client/Label: EMI Records
Artist: Kid Acne
Design: Ben Weaver and Kid Acne
Illustration: Kid Acne
Photography: Sam Ashley/Aurélien Arbet
Country: UK

Physical

We Make It Good

"In true Shilo fashion, this book/DVD is not merely a compilation of the studio's past projects, but rather a thoughtful collection that brings a whole new dimension to the work by show-casing conceptual pieces that both inspired, and were inspired by, the projects themselves," explains Michael Cina. "The disc also offers a rare glimpse into the thought processes of the team in some behind-the-scenes featurettes focused on Shilo's work for Angels & Airwaves, Audio Bullys, and Converse." The idea for this DVD package was to make a book that had shelf life and interest so a hardcover book design was decided on. Helvetica typeface was used throughout.

Product: DVD
Client: YouWorkForThem
Artist: Shilo
Design: WeWorkForThem with Shilo
Country: USA

Beyond the Neighbourhood

South London four-piece band Athlete commissioned Big Active to art direct and design its third album package *Beyond the Neighbourhood.* Having worked on the previous album release, Big Active were keen to produce an intuitive package that visually captured the spirit of the new album in a way that would be bold and striking in an overcrowded market place. "We commissioned illustrator Stevie Gee to create the emblematic cover graphics and illustrations for the booklet which deal with the familiar versus the unfamiliar," explains Gerard Saint. "A spontaneous approach was taken with the imaging to produce an organic and intuitive feel—exploring trains of thought rather than one fixed style or approach." As well as the standard release, a limited-edition hard-back board covered book version was created.

Product: CD
Client/Label: Parlophone Recordings
Artist: Athlete
Art Direction: Gerard Saint/Big Active
Design: Mat Maitland/Big Active
Cover Graphics: Stevie Gee/Stem
Illustration: Stevie Gee/Big Active/Athlete
Country: UK

LoAF01–13

Non-Format designed this series of covers for the release of various artists on the LoAF label, with the brief to produce packaging that would make the LoAF label stand out as an interesting way of distributing music. "We decided that instead of commissioning an illustrator or photographer to produce a cover image for a CD or LP sleeve, we would ask artists and image-makers to provide an image that could be produced as a limited-edition art piece which would then be packaged alongside the music CD with equal status to that of the recording artist," explains Jon Forss. Each release comes with an art print. As the size of the art prints suggested that the packaging needed to be bigger than standard CD packaging, Non-Format chose a 12in format, using a 12in grayboard with a clear plastic document envelope attached to it to hold the art print and CD. The whole package is then screen printed with the recording artist's and visual artist's names in a custom-made typeface. The typeface used is called Udi Dudi and was specially created for the LoAF packaging project. "We wanted something that would look unique to this series and would silk screen well across the grayboard and across the plastic of the bag," adds Forss. "We tried to make the type as big as possible, which accounts for the sometimes awkward line breaks." For LoAF09, Non-Format packaged a 7in single rather than the usual 3in or 5in CDs, so it increased the board size accordingly to a 16½in square board.

Catalog No: LoAF10
Recording Artist: The Lonesomes
Visual Artist: Alan Smithee

Catalog No: LoAF11
Recording Artist: Andrea's Kit
Visual Artist: Grandpeople

Catalog No: LoAF08
Recording Artist: Batfinks
Visual Artist: Hellovon

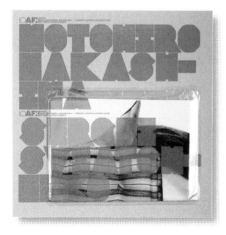

Catalog No: LoAF02
Recording Artist: Motohiro Nakashima
Visual Artist: Sergei Sviatchenko

Catalog No: LoAF04
Recording Artist: Spectac
Visual Artist: Manuel Schibli

Catalog No: LoAF07
Recording Artist: Gavouna
Visual Artist: Athanasios Argianas

Product: CD/Vinyl
Client/Label: LoAF/Lo Recordings
Artist: Various
Design: Non-Format
Countries: UK/USA

Catalog No: LoAF06
Recording Artist: Barbed
Visual Artist: Paul Winstanley

Catalog No: LoAF12
Recording Artist: Kid Twist
Visual Artist: Sam Weber

Catalog No: LoAF09
Recording Artist: Charlie Alex March
Visual Artist: Yokoland

Catalog No: LoAF05
Recording Artist: Vincent Oliver
Visual Artist: Ivan Zouravliov

Catalog No: LoAF01
Recording Artist: Vincent Oliver
Visual Artist: Ivan Zouravliov

Jon Forss
Non-Format
UK/USA

When designing packages for CDs, vinyl, or DVDs what inspires you?
Everything and anything. One thing that rarely influences our design work though is other music packaging. We try not to look at other packaging for inspiration and, as music packaging itself becomes scarcer, this is a temptation that's becoming increasingly easy to resist.

What do you most enjoy about working on such design projects?
Freedom of expression. Music packaging accounts for only a small part of our total workload, and we only take on such projects when we feel we'll be able to experiment and contribute something interesting. As a result we tend to work for small independent labels and, in particular, the UK label Lo Recordings.

Who has been your best client/artist to work with?
When we started out we got a great deal of support from Tony Morley who runs The Leaf Label, but Lo Recordings is the label we've received most commissions from. We've earned an enormous amount of trust from Jon Tye and Gavin O'Shea at Lo over the years, which means we've been offered a great deal of creative freedom and support. We've also been able to have a substantial influence over the visual perception of Lo Recordings and its other labels LoAF and LoEB. It's been very satisfying to see each new piece of packaging becoming part of a larger body of work that represents the visual persona of the label.

What is the most important function for a cover/package to perform? Which ones do you think are particularly successful?
If you take music packaging out of the commercial arena, then there aren't really any essential functions it has to perform (other than to contain the disc or vinyl), but if the packaging has to compete for attention in a record store, I suppose its primary function is to get noticed. The packaging is very often charged with the responsibility of conveying the sound of the music in an environment where it's almost impossible to actually listen to it before buying, so another important function is conveying something of the nature of the music. This is obviously an incredibly subjective point of view and a designer who tries to establish ground rules for genres of music is in danger of resorting to cliché and pastiche, so as a design team, Kjell (Ekhorn) and I have learned to trust our own instincts and pursue our own visual agenda in the hope that the recording artist and record label will empathize with our vision. One yardstick for the power of music packaging would be to take a look at the number of albums I have in my collection that I acquired simply because I liked the look of the packaging.

What is the most interesting piece of packaging you have come across in this area?
I can't choose just one. These sleeves have grabbed my attention: Duran Duran, *Rio*; Björk, *Vespertine*; David Bowie, *Heroes*; Depeche Mode, *Violator*; Durutti Column, *The Guitar and Other Machines*; Fischerspooner, *#1*; Grace Jones, *Living My Life*; Madonna, *American Life*; Massive Attack, *Mezzanine*; New Order, *Blue Monday* (12in); Pink Floyd, *Dark Side of the Moon* and *Wish You Were Here*; Primal Scream, *Exterminator*; Soulwax, *Any Minute Now*; and David Sylvian, *Secrets of the Beehive*. I also love Kim Hiorthøy's sleeves for Rune Grammofon, Vaughan Oliver's for 4AD, Hideki Nakajima's special edition packaging for Ryuichi Sakamoto, and Stefan Gandl's house sleeve for the Detroit Underground label.

What do you think the future holds for music and movie packaging now that so much music (and soon movies) can be downloaded, and how do you think the role of the graphic designer might change?
Buying music on a plastic and metal disc packaged in a plastic case will surely seem ridiculous in a few years' time. It makes much more sense to be able to browse and listen at the same time, which is something that was rarely possible in conventional music stores, and the download obviously offers the possibility of listening to music almost instantly. But music and visuals have such a strong link I can't foresee a time when the two will not be linked in some way. When 5in CD cases replaced 12in LP sleeves, many people saw it as the end of creative music packaging, but that turned out to be far from the truth. Designers had to think on a different scale and many wonderful CD packaging designs were the result. Designers now have to embrace an entirely new medium in order to link music with visual expression. I think moving image is the way things are going. Handheld devices like the iPod are still in their infancy in terms of the storage capacity and access speeds so I think we can expect far more visual content accompanying the music we download in the future. And I suppose the same thing applies to the future of movie packaging. I'm looking forward to it.

Jane Pollard
Beggars Group
UK

What is the most important function for a cover/package to perform?
As more and more of us encounter a flat, small digital image before we handle
the full package (if we do at all), the front cover image is becoming increasingly
important. Once we encounter the package, download the digital booklet, or visit
the website about the release, we should be entering into a space—physical or
digital—that has its own language; it's the contextual space which wraps the
music. Vaughan Oliver's artwork for Scott Walker's album *The Drift* is at once
the most obtuse, intriguing, and accurate visual context there could be for this
incredible album. It acts like a buffer between your reality and the world of the
album. It tells you nothing, but suggests everything that sets your mind in the
right space to receive the music. The designer and programmer Graeme Swinton
then translated this artwork into a digital booklet.

**What is the most interesting piece of packaging you have come
across in this area?**
Another project I was lucky enough to work on was Thom Yorke's album
The Eraser—this had remarkable artwork by Stanley Donwood. The artwork
became the most important and creative aspect of creating an online campaign.
We translated it into a digital space and booklet, we animated it, we inhabited it,
we brought it to life by taking the figure from the cover onto the London streets,
we spread it using cell phones and mapped it across a Google map. The whole
project became in a sense the package for the album.

How do you approach the briefing of designers?
I choose to approach a dialogue with designers in pictures. Take *Silent Sound*,
the project I produced as a visual artist with Iain Forsyth. We commissioned
J. Spaceman to compose a new composition and Chris Bigg from v23 to produce
a brand and a series of artifacts—a program, a CD, a badge, and an invitation.
Our initial question to Chris was how does Silent Sound look? We then started
to pull together images and details, which seemed to communicate the spirit and
intention of the project without prescribing anything about how it might look.
Chris's design was outstanding. It is utterly original, yet feeds in something
of the masonic, retro-futurist, and Victorian reference points we gave him.

**What do you think the future holds for music and movie packaging
now that so much music (and soon movies) can be downloaded, and
how do you think the role of the graphic designer might change
because of this?**
The digital space has the potential to be a brilliantly flexible creative space.
Its lack of parameters can be daunting and we need to move into exploring this
space with the artists and bands working on possibilities collaboratively.

**Have you come across examples of interesting downloadable music
packaging, or any online/interactive elements for music releases?**
This is the area I'm most active in—and it's always a challenge. There are
no set parameters and the way in which we understand and appreciate the
digital space is changing so quickly that no sooner do I feel we've found
a successful approach than it feels out of sync with what we want from this
space. Two projects stick in my mind. The first is one I worked on with Jack
Penate and his first 7in single *Second Minute or Hour* on Young Turks/XL
Recordings. Jack spent 24 hours taking 1,000 Polaroid pictures and having
them taken of him. Then all the Polaroids were signed and numbered, each
unique Polaroid was attached to the front of the 7in single sleeve. We then built
a website that allowed the buyers/collectors of the 7in to claim the copy they
had bought—they could upload a picture of them with their 7in single. The other
project which springs to mind, I didn't work on, but adored. It is a website and
podcast from Nick Cave's Grinderman released on Mute. This website fuelled
my excitement about this project, it gave me a behind-the-scenes insight into
the way the record had come about, it was witty and playful—and it did it all
without compromising the integrity of the band or album.

Contact Details
and
Acknowledgments

Contact Details

±
plusminus.ca
info@plusminus.ca

310k
www.310k.nl
we@310k.nl

344
344design.com
stefan.bucher@344design.com

Abbey Road Interactive
www.abbeyroadinteractive.com
interactive@abbeyroad.com

Dan Abbott
www.axelburger.com
mister.dan@virgin.net

Airside
www.airside.co.uk
anne@airside.co.uk

Alfalfa Studio
www.alfalfastudio.com
ask@alfalfastudio.com

Another Limited Rebellion
www.alrdesign.com
contact@alrdesign.com

David Bailey
www.itsmountpleasant.com
davidmountpleasant@googlemail.com

Big Active
www.bigactive.com
gez@bigactive.com

Chris Bilheimer
www.bilheimer.com
crb@chronictown.com

Bodara
www.bodara.ch
info@bodara.ch

Chris Bolton
www.chrisbolton.org

Jess Bonham
jessbonham.co.uk
jessbonham@yahoo.co.uk

Jon Burgerman
www.jonburgerman.com
fries@jonburgerman.com

Neil Burrell
www.neilburrell.co.uk
neilburrell@gmail.com
blackwhitetoen@googlemail.com

Fabienne Burri
www.c2f.to
to@c2f.to

Matthew Burvill
houseofburvo.co.uk
burvo@houseofburvo.co.uk

C100 Studio
www.c100studio.com
hello@c100studio.com

Cabine
www.cabine.co.uk
rvpol@cabine.co.uk

Jan Oksbøl Callesen
www.janokscal.com
j@janokscal.com
www.gulstue.com
jan@gulstue.com

Dean Chalkley
www.deanchalkley.com
info@deanchalkley.com

Richard Chartier
www.3particles.com
chartier@3particles.com

Deanne Cheuk
www.deannecheuk.com
neomuworld@aol.com

Dom Cooper
www.domcooper.com
domcooperdesign@hotmail.com

Olivier Cornil
www.oliviercornil.be
oc@oliviercornil.be

Cuartopiso
www.cuartopiso.com
info@cuartopiso.com

Ben Curzon
www.bencurzon.com
ben@bencurzon.com

Cyklon
cyklongrafik.net
gytz@cyklongrafik.net

Dimaquina
www.dimaquina.com
info@dimaquina.com

Decoylab
www.decoylab.com
info@decoylab.com

Desorg
www.desorg.cl
flavio@desorg.cl

desres design group
www.desres.de
contact@desres.de

Stanley Donwood
www.slowlydownward.com

Esther de Vries (TM)
www.tm-online.nl
esther@tm-online.nl

Eat Sleep Work/Play
www.eatsleepworkplay.com
mail@eatsleepworkplay.com

Andreas Emenius
www.andreasemenius.com
studio@andreasemenius.com

Emmi
www.emmi.co.uk
hello@emmi.co.uk

Form
www.form.uk.com
studio@form.uk.com

Owen Gildersleeve
www.eveningtweed.com
owen@eveningtweed.com

Grandpeople
www.grandpeople.org
post@grandpeople.org

GraphicTherapy
www.graphictherapy.com
info@graphictherapy.com

Jim Green
www.jimbus.co.uk
jimbus.green@gmail.com

Dominic Harris
www.dominicharris.co.uk
info@dominicharris.co.uk

Jethro Haynes
www.jethrohaynes.com
jethro@jethrohaynes.com

Pete Hellicar
www.petehellicar.com
mail@petehellicar.com

Hudson-Powell
www.hudson-powell.com
studio@hudson-powell.com

Inksurge
www.inksurge.com
broadcast@inksurge.com

Nicole Jacek
nicolejacek@aol.com

Jewboy Corporation™
www.jewboy.co.il
i@jewboy.co.il

Brad Kayal
www.bradkayal.com
me@bradkayal.com

Karlssonwilker Inc.
www.karlssonwilker.com
tellmewhy@karlssonwilker.com

Dylan Kendle
www.dylankendle.com
dylan@tomato.co.uk

Scott King
www.scottking.co.uk
info@scottking.co.uk

David Lane
davidlaneuk.net
dave_lane@mac.com

Joe Lewis
joe-lewis.co.uk
joe@joe-lewis.co.uk

LOVE
www.lovecreative.com
info@lovecreative.com

Lucha Design
www.luchadesign.com
controltower@luchadesign.com

M&E
www.me-me-me.se
info.medesign@gmail.com

Chrissie Macdonald
www.chrissiemacdonald.co.uk
info@chrissiemacdonald.co.uk

Stephane Manel
www.stephanemanel.com
info@stephanemanel.com

Joe Marianek
www.joemarianek.com
joe@joemarianek.com

Peter Maybury
www.softsleeper.com
studio@softsleeper.com

Misprinted Type
www.misprintedtype.com

MusaWorkLab
www.musacollective.com
info@musacollective.com

James Musgrave
www.jamesmusgrave.co.uk
mail@jamesmusgrave.com

Nakajima Design
www.nkjm-d.com
nkjm-d@kd5.so-net.ne.jp

NB: Studio
www.nbstudio.co.uk
mail@nbstudio.co.uk

Richard Niessen (TM)
www.tm-online.nl
richard@tm-online.nl

No Days Off
www.nodaysoff.com
info@nodaysoff.com

Non-Format
www.non-format.com
info@non-format.com

O & E (Oscar Bauer and
Ewan Robertson)
www.oscarandewan.co.uk
mail@oscarandewan.co.uk

Ollystudio (Oliver Walker)
www.ollystudio.co.uk
info@ollystudio.co.uk

Pandarosa
www.pandarosa.net
info@pandarosa.net

Peppered Sprout
pepperedsprout.com
info@pepperedsprout.com

Peter and Paul
www.peterandpaul.co.uk
paul@peterandpaul.co.uk

Garrett Phelan
www.garrettphelan.com
info@garrettphelan.com

pleaseletmedesign
www.pleaseletmedesign.com
oh@pleaseletmedesign.com

Popular (Peter Chadwick)
www.popularuk.com
peter@popularuk.com

Post Typography
www.posttypography.com
info@posttypography.com

Purple Haze Studio
www.thepurplehaze.net
hello@thepurplehaze.net

Qian Qian
www.q2design.com
info@q2design.com

Red Design
www.red-design.co.uk
info@red-design.co.uk

re-public
www.re-public.com
info@re-public.com

Rethink Communications
rethinkcommunications.com
inquiries@rethinkcommunications.com

Cybu Richli
www.c2f.to
to@c2f.to

Paul Roberts
paulroberts.tv
hello@paulroberts.tv

Ewan Robertson
www.oscarandewan.co.uk
ewan@oscarandewan.co.uk

Richard Robinson

Julio Rölle (44flavours)
44flavours.de
hello@44flavours.de

Scott Parker Design
www.scottparkerdesign.co.uk
scott@scottparkerdesign.co.uk

Seripop
www.seripop.com
info@seripop.com

Slang
www.slanginternational.org
nat@slanginternational.org

Laura Snell
laurasnell.co.uk
hello@laurasnell.co.uk

Sopp Collective
www.soppcollective.com
contact@soppcollective.com

Stephen Spyropoulos
www.heavy.com
stephen@heavy.com

Studio Oscar
www.studiooscar.com
info@studiooscar.com

Studio Poana
www.studio-poana.com
contact@studio-poana.com

Sweden Graphics
www.swedengraphics.com
nille@swedengraphics.com

TELA.TV
www.tela.tv
arte@tela.tv

The Small Stakes (Jason Munn)
www.thesmallstakes.com
jason@thesmallstakes.com

Tilt Design Studio

Tyra von Zweigbergk
www.woo.se
tyra@woo.se

us
www.usdesignstudio.co.uk
info@usdesignstudio.co.uk

v23
www.v-23.co.uk
vo@v-23.co.uk

Vår
www.vaar.se
www.woo.se
var@woo.se

Vault49
www.vault49.com
info@vault49.com

Wallzo
www.wallzo.com
studio@wallzo.com

Ben Weaver
selectedprojects.com
ben@selectedprojects.com

WeWorkForThem
www.weworkforthem.com
weare@weworkforthem.com

Steven Wilson
www.wilson2000.com
steve@wilson2000.com

Wiyumi
www.wiyumi.com
go@wiyumi.com

Words Are Pictures
www.wordsarepictures.co.uk
info@wordsarepictures.co.uk

Run Wrake
www.runwrake.com
info@runwrake.com

Zion Graphics
www.ziongraphics.com
ricky@ziongraphics.com

Zip Design
www.zipdesign.co.uk
studio@zipdesign.co.uk

Acknowledgments

I'd like to thank all the designers, art directors, and record labels around the world who took the time and effort to submit work for inclusion in this book. Of course, without your contributions, making this book would not have been possible. Special thanks also to Jon Tye, Ricky Tillblad, Matt Dixon, Patrick Duffy, Jon Forss, and Jane Pollard. Thank you to Lisa Båtsvik-Miller for the design, Simon Punter for the photography, and the continued support of the team at RotoVision.

This book is for Mum.

·Index